A Study of Josef Fuchs' Writings on Human Nature and Morality

David M. O'Leary

UNIVERSITY PRESS OF AMERICA,® INC.
Lanham • *Boulder* • *New York* • *Toronto* • *Oxford*

Copyright © 2005 by
University Press of America,® Inc.
4501 Forbes Boulevard
Suite 200
Lanham, Maryland 20706
UPA Acquisitions Department (301) 459-3366

PO Box 317
Oxford
OX2 9RU, UK

All rights reserved
Printed in the United States of America
British Library Cataloging in Publication Information Available

Library of Congress Control Number: 2005921955
ISBN 0-7618-3130-4 (paperback : alk. ppr.)
ISBN 978-0-7618-3130-3

∞™ The paper used in this publication meets the minimum
requirements of American National Standard for Information
Sciences—Permanence of Paper for Printed Library Materials,
ANSI Z39.48—1992

To ANNIE BLEVINS,

Thank you for keeping me sane all these years,
but most of all,
thank you for being a dear friend

Contents

Introduction and Chapter Outlines		vii
I	The Human Person exists as the Image of God	1
II	The Immutable Being of the Human Person is Basically Mutable	7
III	The Human Person Exists With the Capacity of Self-realization	13
IV	Basic Freedom and Basic Conscience	19
	A. Basic Freedom	19
	B. Conscience	24
	C. Relationship of Basic Freedom and Basic Conscience	29
V	God's Salvation in Jesus Christ is the Genuine Morality	37
VI	Natural Law and Moral Norms	47
VII	Human Acts and Their Values	57
VIII	Fundamental Option	65
Bibliography		73
About the Author		75

Introduction and Chapter Outlines

This book is a study of Josef Fuchs' writings on the topic of human nature and morality. First, this will not be a chronological study of the development of Fuchs' thoughts in moral theology as his range of interests have varied. This is not to say that the author has not been coherent and consistent throughout his career. He has repeated quite a number of topics and concerns in published texts, such as: The human person is the image of God, The human person is called by Christ in the midst of his/her human life, sin is a complete "human no" to God and to Christ, etc.

The writings of Fuchs can be divided into three main categories: his responses to the controversial issues which he has been confronted with, the additions to his previous viewpoints in his on going effort of understanding the phenomenon of human existence, and the synthesis of the two. Due to the fact of Fuchs' continuous process of synthetically understanding of human nature and its vocation towards perfection, it would be superficial to trace back successively all of his analytically developed thoughts on the issues of human nature and morality.

This thesis is not a complete study of Fuchs' writings since Josef is still living, writing and developing his theology of ethics. I believe Fuchs would not want his writings to be a moral conclusion; rather they should be a springboard for further thought in the area of moral theology. Fuchs' ethics are based on Sacred Scriptures and Roman Catholic teachings. Fuchs is always inviting his readers to discover insights into human existence and to explore the phenomenon of human nature within the gracious effectiveness of Christ's Incarnation.

The first half of this book (Chapters I–IV) will show Fuchs' understanding of human nature. Fuchs has a dynamic view of human nature. And it is this dynamic or mutable nature of human existence which is the motivation for Fuchs to write his own ethics. In order to understand Fuchs' view of morality, one has to first understand his view of human nature and the underlying issues of basic freedom and basic conscience.

The second half of this book (Chapters V–VIII) will show the type of morality Fuchs offers within his understanding of human nature. Issues to be addressed will be; God's salvation in Jesus Christ as the foundation for a genuine morality, natural law and moral norms, human acts and their values, and fundamental option.

The procedure by which Fuchs' writings are used in this book should be outlined. As mentioned above, this is not meant to be a chronological study. And one should argue that Fuchs should not be held accountable for his older views on certain issues. The opposite of this objection is a target of this study, namely, to see the on going development of Fuchs' writings in light of new insights from the social sciences. Most of Fuchs' writings are found in articles in theological journals. Several major texts have also been published. An outline of this book by chapters may help the reader to grasp the scope of this study.

CHAPTER I OF PART ONE ON HUMAN NATURE

The human person exists as the image of God. Human nature is seen as fallen yet elevated by the redemption of Christ. Fuchs rendered this biblical definition of human existence with his polemical view saying that "man's nature is not the work of sin",[1] (*Natural Law*, p. 59). Fuchs begins his definition of human existence with the opposite viewpoint of Protestant theologians who hold that the human race has been corrupted ever since the time of original sin. The main idea behind this issue for Fuchs is that human nature is still redeemable by God and in the process of dynamically self-realization in one's own self, and the self-responsibility to the call of Christ in this world. To Fuchs this is "the clear doctrine of Holy Scripture" (*Natural Law*, p. 61).

The image of God in human nature is proprium and *alienum* at the same time (*Natural Law*, p. 63). This image of God is the basic foundation for the knowledge of morality; yet without this basic foundation, human existence can still achieve some knowledge of morality in his or her attitude of being an autonomous human person.

We will discuss at length this part of the biblical definition with further issues as: why Fuchs begins his understanding of human nature with a biblical definition, and what this definition aims at in his career of writings.

II. THE IMMUTABLE BEING OF THE HUMAN PERSON IS BASICALLY MUTABLE

The human person exists with his or her nature which is immutable and yet dynamic within the historicity of mankind and the history of salvation. This is not to say that human nature is immutable in essence and yet mutable in accidents. This is quite different from the Greek and Medieval traditions on the notion of human nature. This makes Fuchs stand so unique in his writings. For Fuchs human nature is historical! It is simply because human nature in each individual is a personal nature.[2] The human person is not only responsible for being open to the changes of his/her own "given existence," but also for effecting and conducting these changes. Each individual person exists as a responsible creature with regard to the nature of the person and that world. For Fuchs, human nature is not simply a composite of body and soul which exists without regard to the effects of time and space but an essence that is creatively progressive in its paradoxical structure, which includes the mutable and immutable phenomena. Fuchs believes that human nature has its own clear and distinct characteristic, without which human nature would not be human. This distinct character is the phenomenon of self-realization in each human person. Yet what is this self-realization? This question will be answered in Chapter II.

The paradoxical phenomenon of immutability and mutability in human nature will be explored. We will see why Fuchs views human nature as "being and becoming," and what purpose this viewpoint will serve in his writings on morality. In the discussion of the mutability of human nature, we will also analyze the causes and effects of this mutability in the human person as well as its proper direction. Further exploration will be given to the question whether mutability is possible in any human person with regard to the level of consciousness of each person. Chapter II clarifies Fuchs' specific viewpoint on the dynamic nature of the human person.

III. THE HUMAN PERSON EXISTS WITH THE CAPACITY OF SELF-REALIZATION

The human person exists with the capacity of self-realization (*Gesinnung*) which basically means the "self" with its free attitudes (c.f. *Christian Morality*, p. 106). Fuchs begins his understanding of self-realization by distinguishing his own views from those of humanistic psychologists.[3] To Fuchs self-realization is yielding to the process of seeking one's self.

According to Fuchs this phenomenon (*Gesinnung*) of human nature has three aspects: "responsible self-realization," "self-realization as radical openness," and "vertical self-transcendence as self-realization." The first term is basic and all all-inclusive task of each individual. The first task of self-realization is subjectively conscious. For Fuchs it manifests and cooperates with the insights of evaluating reason (such as *bonum hominis est secundun rationem* esse) to the extent that "reason has the possibility of arriving at self-understanding and also at an understanding of individual realities."[4]

The second term, "self-realization as radical openness," is horizontal. It has to do with the openness in three areas of human reality;

> openness to the facts and human meaning of the horizontal reality that belongs to our self, openness to what is unconditioned in conditioned human reality, and openness to the other in interpersonal relationships.[5]

The third term, "vertical self-transcendence as self-realization," is the ultimate self-realization which consists in transcendence towards what is absolutely transcendent, namely God. For Fuchs this last term is the most important in the sense that it enables each person to reach the perfection of human nature. Yet how can each person reach this kind of self-transcendence? This question will be answered in Chapter III.

The relationship of these three terms of self-realization will be discussed. Chapter III will analyze why Fuchs believes that the "vertical self-transcendence" is so important for his ethics. We will discuss the opposite aspect of this threefold of *Gesinnung*, namely, self-alienation. We will see how Fuchs states his ideas on the negative part of human nature, and why he uses it to intensify the positive of the threefold terms of human self-ealization. Chapter III will be related to the first two chapters and how this idea of self-realization modifies the meaning of human nature.

IV. BASIC FREEDOM AND BASIC CONSCIENCE

The human person exists with his or her "transcendent freedom" and "conscience" which are essential forces and motives for their creative and progressive lives towards the perfection of humanness. Chapter IV will explore the meaning and relationships between basic freedom and basic conscience.

Transcendent freedom is a basic freedom which enables each person to determine himself or herself totally as a person. This kind of freedom, inasmuch as one commits one's self as a person, takes place at the center of the person even though it expresses and realizes itself in and through certain acts and deeds. This fundamental free disposition of each person for Fuchs is primary; and if there are any judgments about moral acts, they must be made only in the context in which the acts truly express this real commitment of the person in basic freedom.[6]

The first half of Chapter IV will discuss the relationship of the exercise of basic freedom and the categorical freedom of choices of the human person. Also, we will explore how Fuchs can be certain about the knowledge of each human person on this basic freedom. We will treat this topic of transcendent freedom in relationship with Fuchs' understanding of "fundamental option." But in the first part of this book treatment of fundamental freedom will only be a minor part. A full treatment of this topic will be given in the second four chapters of this book. The second half of Chapter IV will explore the meaning of conscience.

The human person exists with a conscience which is experienced as the absolute relationship with the Absolute, i.e. God. This basic or fundamental phenomenon of conscience for Fuchs is transcendental freedom and the source of personal decisions. In addition to this meaning, conscience can also be experienced as a particular-categorical source for particular acts. Fuchs stresses that this second meaning of conscience is not absolute, but rather objectively fallible. These are the "subjective" and "objective" meanings of conscience. Fuchs also gives an elaborate treatment to the phenomenon to conscience and its relation with the many realities of human person such as: conscience and orientation for the conduct of life, conscience and practical reason, conscience and religious experience, conscience and superego ethical maturity and ethical immaturity. I will condense Fuchs' treatment of conscience into two meanings; the subject-orientation of the conscience, and the object-orientation of the conscience.[7]

The second half of Chapter IV will explore the term "conscience." Fuchs' understanding of the nature of human conscience and its role in his writings will be shown. Since conscience and transcendental freedom have a close relationship in the inner reality of the human person, we will explore this relationship in-depth. Conscience and transcendental freedom also help the human person to live and act fully. The last section of Chapter IV will discuss the complicated issue of how "conscience" stands in relationship with "the authority" and "the positive law." We will see whether conscience is relative to them or should it be the other way around. We will address the difficulty of our understanding of conscience with the pluralistic conditions of human society.

PART TWO: A MORALITY FOR THE ABOVE NOTION OF HUMAN NATURE

Having established an understanding of human nature for Fuchs, we can begin to address the question of morality, which is conditioned by his dynamic view of human nature. A caution needs to be given before we look for the ethics Fuchs' uses. One needs to keep in mind the distinction that is made between "personal morality" and "right behavior."

The latter is merely a study of the categorical deeds or actions of a human person, which for Fuchs is not sufficient for any attempt to understand the ethical values of the whole human person. The former is more important.

It is a study of the "moral person" with regard to the whole involvement of the moral person in his or her transcendental freedom through its exercise in the categorical actions. Fuchs is more interested in the former. He shows how this is the position of the Second Vatican Council in Christian Morality, pp. 19–27. He even tries to convince his readers that "personal morality" is the message and the call of God in the New Testament, i.e. for the human person to live a life of "bearing fruit."[8]

A major exploration of "personal morality" will take place since it will serve to reveal a certain morality based upon the findings in part one of this book, on human nature. In this second part of the book, we will show Fuchs' understanding of "right behavior," and we will show the relationship between "personal morality" and "right behavior."

Finally, a synthesis of parts one and two of this book will be made. The purpose being to discover whether Fuchs' view of human nature and morality are applicable to the human person or not. An outline of Chapters V–VIII may further help the reader understand the scope of this book.

V. GOD'S SALVATION IN JESUS CHRIST IS GENUINE MORALITY

This chapter will show the call of God for the human person and its manifest effectiveness through the incarnational redemption of Christ. The human person is called by God on "whose being" the human person has depended and participated in ever since creation took place. The discussion in this chapter is based on the biblical image of human nature. We will discuss the effects of Christ's grace on human nature and see why Fuchs prefers to begin his discussion of ethics with the vocation of God for the human person. The first four chapters are balanced with the second four chapters, so some points may be repeated to show this connection.

VI. NATURAL LAW AND MORAL NORMS

This chapter will explore natural law and positive law in relation to the mutable character of human nature. We will discuss the values and the absoluteness as well as the universality of natural law and that of positive law. This chapter we will show how Fuchs sees the values of the laws must be evolved with the historical character of human nature. We will analyze the function of natural law and that of positive law, and show how these two laws have a dominant role in Fuchs' writings.

VII. HUMAN ACTS AND THEIR VALUES

Human acts and moral values both in transcendental intentionality and in the categorical behavior. Chapter VII will explore the distinction between the pre-moral values and the moral values, as well as the distinction between moral goodness and moral rightness. We will study the nature of human acts in relation to the idea of "responsible self-realization" in the inner realities of the human person. A close analysis will be given to the distinction and relationship between the transcendental and categorical norms.

VIII. FUNDAMENTAL OPTION

Fundamental option and the "law of Christ" in relation to the transcendental freedom and the conscience of the human person. Chapter VIII will explore the role of Christ as the motif and the final purpose of the ethical life of each person. This chapter will cover the basic choice of the human person which cannot be arbitrary. This choice of the human person is either positive or negative to the call of Christ. Chapter VIII will show how Fuchs states this either/or choice is central for human transcendental freedom and how each person can truly make this choice by one's fundamental option.

NOTES

1. For this study preference will be given to the term "human" over "man" with the intention to express inclusively both female and male genders. Even Fuchs has this intention in his recent writings. Let us also remember that the term "man" in its Anglo Saxon background had meant "one" which included both "she" and "he". To Fuchs the inclusiveness of the term "human" does not merely refer to the two genders of human existence, but also to whoever exists as the image of God, viz., both believers and non-believers inasmuch as they exist in the form of human being. Let us keep in mind this important issue in order to study Fuchs' work correctly.
2. The Absoluteness of Behavioral Moral Norms, p. 127.

3. To humanistic psychologists, the human self is unequivocally reduced to psychological health and integration, as well as the other manifold aspects of human reality; including culture, ethics and religions.
4. *Christian Morality*, p. 148.
5. *Ibid.*
6. *Human Values and Christian Morality*, p. 99.
7. *Christian Morality*, pp. 118–132.
8. *Christian Morality*. pp. 150–153.

Chapter I

The Human Person exists as the Image of God

Among the many approaches toward understanding the nature of "human person" Fuchs' begins with the biblical definition, "man is an image of God" (Gen. 1:26).[1] By placing human nature in real contact with the creator, Fuchs wants to affirm its goodness and its undubitable ground to the extent that the "human person" receives its own existence directly from God, and that it is not "the work of sin."[2]

Genesis 1:26 allows Fuchs to develop his understanding of the relational dimension of human nature: the human being is not merely natural. It exists in a relation to its ground which is God.[3] This fundamental relation suggests that human nature belongs to both the natural and supernatural orders. The theological distinction between natural and supernatural orders. The theological distinction between natural and supernatural does not imply that the human person exists as a purely natural entity. Rather it simply serves to emphasize that the human person "in his/her total existence is and always has been directed positively to a supernatural end."[4] One can draw from Fuchs' understanding of human nature as being relational that the human person exists primarily and totally as an ethical being. That is to say the human person in Fuchs' theology comes into being simultaneously at both ontological and ethical levels. The ontological level simply means that the human person was created by God as His likeness; while its ethical level expresses the enormous fact that the human person owes its being from God in such a way that it must live toward the perfection of its source. Due to the effect of original sin, an objection here emerges as to how ontological it remains and how ethical it can be within its fallen condition. The response to this objection will be illustrated through analyzing the what of human nature, the how of its becoming, an d the why of its presence. Let us consider each in particular.

To present his theology of human nature, Fuchs reviews the traditional teaching of the Catholic Church on the world and humankind with regard to the effect of original sin. "The consequence of (original) sin is the loss of preternatural and supernatural grace but this loss leaves nature as such untouched."[5] This is the positive view of Fuchs' theology of human nature. The effect of original sin did not destroy the original state of human nature; rather, it effected the human person in such a way that the person lost the original condition of being in the "hand in hand" type of relationship with God.[6] In other words, it did not make the human person become an inhuman being. Fuchs did not here offer a clear and sufficient analysis about the effects of original sin. He only follows what the Catholic Church has already stated.

> Certainly man is now a sinner; original sin entered the first man and remains in all his descendants. We must be aware also of personal sin and of all the consequences of both, which mankind in the present economy has to bear. It is quite possible to distinguish, . . ., the reality which we call "nature" does not have its origin in the sin of man but comes directly from the hands of God. God speaks through it and reveals himself in it. It bears his features and it is his image. How could it be otherwise since nature is the creature of God?[7]

If "nature with the consequences of original sin still has its ontological ground in God, so does human nature. It is simply because human nature remains as a creature of God, and "being a creature always includes being made in God's image."[8] Fuchs believes that the human being within the surrounding world is indeed the demand of God. Since the human being was demanded by God in creation, it must be proprium and alienum at the same time. That is to say, human nature must be proper to God's being in its sharing in the divine image, and at the same time it must be different from his being in being a creature. It must be reasoned that the human being must bear these two qualities simultaneously. Otherwise:

> "a pure proprium would exclude the created likeness to God and a pure alienum would imply a false nominalism. This would inevitably imply a denial of the earnestness of God's love."[9]

According to Fuchs' theology this is the nature of the human person. It is a revelation of God and of His will; thus, it has an ontological likeness to God even though it remains as a creature within the consequence of sin.

Because the human person was created by God, certainly it exists "only through God's love."[10] God's love creates its own object which is the human person. Yet the human person is not merely an indifferent correlative fact of God's creating love. It is rather an image of God's glory which God embraces in his love.[11] The human person in itself is truly the love of God. The human person stems entirely from God in such a way that all it can offer to God as His created image is entirely the love of God itself. This is how the human person comes into being according to Fuchs. This theological explanation (of how the human person was created) is quite consistent to the analysis of human ontological likeness to God, which has been just mentioned.

Being an object of God's love is the ethical attribute of human nature, which presupposes the ontological likeness to God. By ethical attribute, we simply mean the goodness of God's love as manifest in human nature. This ethical attribute in the inner core of the human person enables him/herself to realize that he/she by nature belongs to the good which is not merely of his/her created being, but also of the living love of the Creator.

From the viewpoint of traditional metaphysics, by all means "being" in itself is always "the good."[12] However, within the context of admitting the presence of sin in human nature and in its surrounding world, there should be a distinction of ontological level from ethical level in the human nature itself. Fuchs posits this distinction for his ethics. It does not divide human nature into two distinctive degrees of being. It simply serves to clarify the ground of human being and the enfeeblement of the human person after the original sin has occurred. The ethical level of human nature is the ground for Fuchs' ethics of homo viator, namely, that of human person on his/her way to God. The theological treatment of homo viator will be mentioned in our next discussion of the present purpose of the human being as the likeness to God in its own world and in the world surrounding.

> Since God created man as we actually find him, (as fallen) all that is good for man is determined by God's nature and this remains the case as long as man remains man.[13]

In order to present the purpose of the human being in creation, Fuchs reminds his readers that it is naturally impossible to envisage human nature as detached from the activity and the love of God. Even that God created human nature out of nothing (ex nihilo), this very fact is the reason to acknowledge and to admit that human nature comes continually and entirely from the glory of the divine being. If one cannot envisage human nature detached from God's activity, one must accept the fact that the human person as the likeness of God has a relationship to the world. The human person is God's partner in His providence to the extent that he/she must develop and humanize his/her own self and the given realities of the world.[14] Thus the human person is a responsible being for the world surrounding it and for its own world. It cannot exist as an indifferent being, nor can it merely be an instrumental being for the reality of God's image. Since the "human being" derives entirely from God, it must exist in such a way that it is obliged to live its life as coming from God. Fuchs even concludes that the image of God in human nature "becomes with undeniable necessity the God-given norm of the life of the spiritual man."[15] That is to say the ontological likeness to God is the divine given norm for the human person itself. Fuchs uses the formulation homo viator to express the phenomenon of human response to such a divine given norm, namely, the human person is on its way to God. Yet what is it this phenomenon of homo viator in the human person? This is the ethical dimension of the human person.

Fuchs responds to the question that it is the vocation of God for the human person in the present order of salvation. The call is realized "concretely in Christ's gracious act of Redemption."[16] Fuchs even argues that this vocation, as a necessarily gracious act of God, is the epitome of His faithfulness to humankind. Fuchs holds this point of view because he believes that the human person can hardly come to a total decision, which concerns the wholeness of the person itself in one single temporal act. In other words, the vocation for the wholeness of the human person must be determined by the totality of its deeds, and activities. Fuchs also renders the unmistaken words of Revelation to say that the human person cannot be himself/herself change the aversion from God through sin (if there being committed any in a single temporal act) into conversion to God. Thus Fuchs concludes that it is God who in fact "sustains the human person homo viator in spite of sin, so that we have contact with God through the Redemption in Christ—in time and eternity."[17] To Fuchs, homo viator is the true meaning and purpose of the human being in spite of the presence of individual sin and the all embracing sin of Adam.

The theology of homo viator plays an important role in Fuchs' ethics. He wants to understand human nature in the context of concrete history and the history of salvation. To Fuchs the human person is a historical being. It endures the dynamics of the history into which it participates, and the vocation of God in salvific history to which it offers its responsible responses in return. Human nature is historical in its dynamic character, if there is any, it is so simply because it derives its being from the living God who shares His own love and reveals that love in human nature.

NOTES

1. *Natural Law: A Theological Investigation*, pp. 59–84. This is Fuchs' polemical theology against the thought of some Protestant theologians (contemporary with Fuchs' early writing career), which considered "human likeness to God" merely in relation with God, and not as an ontological likeness of God's divine being. In the context of Natural Law, Fuchs is not interested in an exegesis of the background of Gen. 1:26. He merely takes this definition from the Catholic tradition. His intention here is

to posit a ground for his theology of "Natural Law," the meaning of which we will discuss in due time. One should also keep in mind the words of V. Rad on the statement "Let us make man in our image," "This is no freely ventured theologoumenon," namely it is not freely taken as the saying of God. (*Theological Dictionary of the New Testament*, Vol. II, ed. By Kittel, p. 390). In Chapter V, we will see Fuchs' extensive interpretation of the image of the human person, as well as his analysis of the image of God.

2. *Natural Law*, p. 59. In this book, the terms "human person" and "human existence" will be used interchangeably. The reason for this will be clear in Part II. With regard to the issue of inclusive language, I will be using the terms" man/woman, he/she, him/her, himself/herself, and his/her. To Fuchs the inclusiveness of the term "human" or "man" in his writings does not merely focus on the two genders of human existence. Rather, it expressly signifies whoever exists as the image of God, viz., both believers and non-believers inasmuch as they exist in the form of the human being. As Fuchs says, "when I say man, I always mean humanity-society." Personal Responsibility, p. 178.

3. *Natural Law*, pp. 42, 60.

4. Ibid, p. 44.

5. *Natural Law*, p. 59.

6. The phrase "hand in hand" is rendered from Gen. 2:15, which expresses the interpersonal relationship of God and Adam. The citation reads "The Lord God took the man and put him in the garden of Eden to till it and keep it." All of the Scripture quotations in this book are taken from *The New Oxford Annotated Bible*, ed. by May & Metzger (New York: Oxford University Press, 1977).

7. *Natural Law*, p. 60. This quotation serves to emphasize Fuchs' connection that the present condition of "nature" has its root not in "sin" but directly in the creative hands of God.

8. *Natural Law*, p. 60.

9. Ibid., p. 63.

10. Ibid.

11. Here Fuchs quotes from Paul's theology in 1 Cor. 11:7 and from James' in Jas. 3:9, the notion that humankind is the image and the glory of God.

12. The term "being" here is used in the sense of a created being, which has its source from the divine being who is Esse bonum, Esse purum, Esse tantum (Aquinas, *Suma Theologies*, Q. 5, 6). Even though Fuchs did not quote explicitly from Aquinas in classroom lectures, references were made to Aquinas' thought as traditional teaching of Catholicism. But there is a difference between Fuchs' use of the term being and Aquinas. Fuchs uses the term in a more phenomenological tradition, which is not the same as the Medieval way of doing metaphysics. But both theologians agree that being is a good in itself, because all being draws its source from God who is good in Himself and in creation.

13. *Natural Law*, p. 67 (as fallen) my addition.

14. In Part II of this book, we shall have occasion to return to the discussion of "humanizing progress."

15. *Natural Law*, p. 64.

16. *Ibid.*, p. 83.

17. Further discussion on homo viator will be given in Chapter VIII on fundamental option. Let us bear in mind that "the human person on its way to redemption," to Fuchs is the property of the sinner as well as of Christians. It is the right of humankind in the simple sense of the term even though the human person exists within the presence of sin. Even in the case of a sinner, Fuchs firmly holds that God still grants the sinner this call and the possibility of striving towards God. It is not surprising to see that Fuchs holds this positive viewpoint on human nature if we have studied his theological treatment on original sin, saying that "the consequence of sin is the loss of supernatural grace but . . . leaves nature as such untouched." Natural Law, p. 59.

Chapter II

The Immutable Being of the Human Person is Basically Mutable

In Chapter I, we arrived at the notion that the human being is the image of God. It is responsible and historical being. Fuchs emphasizes that the human being is not merely a "datum" (a given being), but also a "task" (munus).[1] It is the task that the human person, finding itself in various conditions and situations, must search for and make its "datum" a new and more suitable reality. Since it is a task, the human person is not simply a static being. Fuchs now introduces a new perception of the human being which includes both "immutability" and the "mutability" of the human person. For clarification of this complicated perception of the human being, Fuchs offers three analytical arguments:

> In the first place, the state of being man does not exclude that the human state may differ in different epochs and cultures, just as it is actualized in different individuals and life situations without placing man's nature in question . . . For even that which essentially constitutes man, that which therefore belongs unalterably to his nature, as also his permanent structure, is basically mutable.
>
> Second, the question of mutability-immutability is connected with man's historicity. History is possible only in virtue of the mutability of that which remains ever the same. Now man is an historical being, not only in terms of the successive variations of past, present and future, but above all, in the sense that man himself designs and brings to realization the plot-lines of his given existence and its progress into the future . . . , he becomes to an ever increasing degree a different person.
>
> Third, mutability and historicity are connected with the fact that man is person and nature in one. Person and nature can be placed counter to each other, so that, nature expresses the intrapersonal given of man and his world, while person represents the I, possessing and shaping itself in terms of the given nature. However, one's personhood also is given and in this sense it is nature, indeed

the determining elements of one's humanness, and in all this sense of human nature. The man consists above in his being a person (i.e. possessing ratio).[2]

What does all this mean? How should we understand this phenomenon that mutability belongs to the immutable essence of the human person? Obviously, Fuchs does not repeat the traditional metaphysical view of the immutable attributes of the human being, neither does he regard the self-evident distinction in its structure, namely between the universality of human nature (intellectual being) and the individuality of the human person (individualized rational agent). Let us consider these three citations, each by itself. It would be helpful to begin with the third one.

All of these three arguments appear with the presupposition that the human being is historical. In the paragraph cited above, Fuchs stresses that the human being consists above all in its being a person. In other words, the personhood is the most essential attribute to specify the human being. If the specification of the human being depends on its personhood, there is no wonder that Fuchs holds person and nature to be one entity.

As we have seen in the above section, Fuchs defines the human being as a relational being. It is related to its creator, to its own world, and to the world surrounding. Plainly, if the human being is relational, there remains only one way to comprehend such a relational dimension of the human being, i.e. that of its personhood. Since the human being is a responsible creature (for the development of its own being and of the world), the most practical way to understand it as such is to speak of it in terms of personhood. Only when one presupposes the presence of the person can one speak of its responsibility. Yet, these two reasons are merely mechanical from the viewpoint of the epistemological approach. They do not help to clarify sufficiently our concerns of the complicated structure of the human being. How does Fuchs understand the term "person?"

Fuchs believes the person is "an individual and is the subject both of his free moral goodness and of his right conduct in the world."[3] This is the most explicit statement of Fuchs' notion on human person. Yet, he only gives an ethically operational definition of the term person. Elsewhere, Fuchs repeats that "man, experienced as a gift and as commission, is a person. That is, he is in himself, as conscious of himself, deciding about himself, disposing of himself, summoned."[4]

For Fuchs, the person is the most essential manifestation of human existence. But he does not offer a sufficient understanding of the reality in human existence, which is called person. We do not see Fuchs holding that personality as the fundamental being of the human species, neither do we discern Fuchs' saying all reality is personal. Fuchs does combine human nature with the human person in one "humanness" or human entity for human existence, and that in this one humanness "person" is the most authentic disclosedness of human existence. The reason why Fuchs spends so much time combining nature and person in one "humanness" will be discussed in Chapter VII. Let us return to his argument on the mutability and immutability of human existence.

In the third citation, Fuchs makes a double argument to support his view on the mutability of the human being. In fact, it is a tautological demonstration. He posits a primary premise which places human nature and the human person in contrast to each other as a dichotomy. He then encompasses these two human realities into one entity which he calls "one humanness." Human nature expresses the intrapersonal reality of human existence, whereas, the person is that which represents the I and shapes itself via nature. This "I" however is also a given reality (from the viewpoint of the theology of creation which holds that everything that exists is a being created by God); it should and must, therefore, be considered as nature. Given this demonstration, a couple of remarks should be made for this tautological argument.

First, from the viewpoint of linguistic consideration, perhaps Fuchs wants to correct all of the traditional ways of understanding the relation between nature and person. Person and nature, strictly speaking, are dialectically antithetical and progressing into the synthetic sublatum which is in Fuchs' terms the one humanness. In this progress into the synthetic sublatum, the person plays the major role over and against nature. Fuchs wants to say that the human person possesses and shapes itself via nature to ever increasing degrees a different person.

We have seen that human existence for the most part discloses itself as a person. In the simple sense, the term "person" suggests the "who" of that person, which in turn denotes the uniqueness and individuality of the person. If one speaks of the uniqueness of a being, one must do so in terms of its duration and history. This is what Fuchs does in the second citation. The human person is a historical being. It is historical in both the external spacio-temporal conditions and the internal structures or the depth dimension of the person. To Fuchs, the latter is more important for it is the process of continuous realization in which the person designs itself towards future for being ever more increasingly a different person. Thus, the human person is basically historical in terms of the mutability of that which remains ever the same. Plainly, without the movement and the mutability of a person there would be no history of that person. This is a simple fact. But what kind of history does Fuchs mean?

Fuchs uses the term "progress" to convey his understanding of history.

> As being in history, we cannot adopt a static attitude; we have to be incessantly making plans for the future. . . the future of humanity following on after us. So

we must always attend, as our most specific duty, to the development of our own persons, of the human world around us and of the world in the service of mankind.[5]

Fuchs now introduces us to the specific duty of humanity in which all human beings must develop their own persons as well as the world surrounding them. To Fuchs, this duty is a requirement of God from creation. Yet could wonder how and in what way does a human person develop itself? Fuchs responds;

the fact that man—as the image of God—is a person means not merely that he can accept, preserve, contemplate mankind, the world of men and himself as a given reality, but rather that he should grasp it, have control over it, shape it, develop it, increasingly and in a more active fashion stamp it with his own nature—in other words increasingly humanize it.[6]

For Fuchs, to be a person is to have the most specific duty of developing both the personal self and the world surrounding this self by humanizing them. This progress of humanization is possible because the human being is a personal and historical being. Fuchs affirms that any progress that is not truly human and in opposition to a real moral order, is not progress at all.[7] To humanize both the person and the world is to realize oneself as a person, both in the horizontal relationship with other fellow-persons and in the vertical relationship with God. Fuchs concludes, only when one continues to achieve this humanizing progress, does one fulfill the mandate of creation. This is how Fuchs understands the term "history." It is the history, after having been created by God, which is continuously moving with the major effect being the totality of the "personal being," who has an ethical mandate to control this history and to make it become human.

Thus for Fuchs, "history" can no longer be distinguished between the history of the secular world and the subjective reality of the human being. It is an anthropologically centered history in which the "person" of the human being is the controller of all, i.e. of its own self and of the world. In the above third citation, Fuchs combines nature and person in one humanness. Fuchs now synthesizes the history of the world with that of human being into one "humanizing progress." If this is how Fuchs views history and the human person, there is no wonder that the Fuchs stresses the mutability of the human person. The first citation above serves as the conclusion of Fuchs' analysis on the mutable characteristic of the human being. Fuchs understands the personhood of the human beings in terms of the ethical context, namely, in its responsibility to humanize the created world. This understanding of the personhood is different from the traditional viewpoint, which simply held that the person is rational essence in individual substance. It follows that Fuchs has a different understanding of the human being that is the immutable essence of the human being is basically mutable. Our arguments with Fuchs so far supports this new concept of the human being. Yet the paradoxical structure of this important conclusion (i.e. the mutability basically belongs to the immutable essence of the human being) deserves a few remarks from the viewpoints of epistemology and ontology.

Basically speaking, the content and the structure of the statement itself is an oxymoron, namely, it is a dictum in which the opposite ideas (of mutability and immutability) are combined. It is hard to see how persuasive and convincing Fuchs can be in such a statement. The problem lies in the fact that Fuchs uses the traditional language of metaphysics to express his phenomenological perception of human existence. It is difficult to accept this fact if one prefers to consider Fuchs as a responsible writer. In other words, if Fuchs wants to express his unique notion of human being, he should do so in his own terminology. In a sense, the above dictum can be rephrased like this: the human being, even though coming into existence in its immutable essence, remains as yet continuously becoming an ever new person. Or another way to express it, the human being is perpetually disclosing itself towards the entelechy or the perfection of its personhood. Only by articulating in this way can one retain the immutable essence of human existence and simultaneously acknowledge the historical fact of its personal development.

If one places the above dictum in the context of ontology, one cannot deny the fact that Fuchs is not interested in the "to be" as such in his analysis of human being. In this case, a reference to the German term "Dasein" would be helpful. In phenomenological tradition "Dasein" means being-here-and-now, which signifies human existence. "Dasein" receives it being from its source "Sein" (which can be translated pure Being or the house of beings). Besides disclosing itself as "dasein," "Sein" also unfolds itself as "Seindes," which is the beingness of all things in the world. Thus the furthest back which a phenomenologist can reach to the purse "to be" is to refer to the being as such or the house of beings, namely "Sein."[8] If "Being as such" is so creative in its disclosedness in "dasein" and in "Seindes," there would hardly remain any concept of immutability for any beings in the perceptive mind of the phenomenologists. In addition, ever since the time of Immanuel Kant, "Dasein," though meaning human being-here-and-now, has been articulated in the ethical context, that is, it has meant the moral person.

I believe Fuchs uses the term "Dasein" or "Menchsein" in a different context from the phenomenological tradition, and defines "Dasein" as the image of God. The "Dasein" or "Menchsein" of Fuchs' writings, as presented thus far, is basically a person and it is creative in its self-development. This is why a review of its phenomenological background is worthy for our interpretation of Fuchs' belief in the mutability of human existence.

In summary, the human being of Fuchs' ethics is basically a historical person who exists with a moral duty to humanize itself and the world. Because of this the human being can no longer be considered as a static or immutable entity. Rather the human person is engaged in the progression toward the fulfillment of the external conditions as well as the depth dimension of the human person itself. To Fuchs, the external realities of the human person are categorical, and the depth dimension is transcendental. To humanize is to self-realize the totality of the person in these two domains. In Fuchs' understanding it is the self-realization in both the horizontal and vertical relations of the human person as the responsible creature of the historical creation. In the next chapter, I will move the discussion to the personal self-realization.

NOTES

1. "Morality as the shaping of the Future of Man, in *Personal Responsibility*, p. 177.
2. "The Absoluteness of Behavioral Moral Norms, in *Personal Responsibility*, pp. 126–127.
3. "Morality: Person and Acts", in *Christian Morality*, p. 108.
4. "Nature and Culture in Bioethics," in *Christian Ethics in a Secular Arena*, p. 93.
5. "On the Theology of Human Progress," *Human Values and Christian Morality*, p. 183.
6. "On the Theology of Human Progress," *Christian Values and Christian Morality*, p. 182.
7. Ibid. p. 186.
8. Martin Heidegger, *Being and Time*, trans. By Macquarrie and Robinson (New York, 1962), part one.

Chapter III

The Human Person Exists With the Capacity of Self-realization

Fuchs begins his understanding of "self-realization" by distinguishing his own view from those of the humanistic psychologists and those of some philosophers. Fuchs uses the term "Gesinnung" to signify the human self. "Gesinnung" means the self with its free attitudes in the totality of the human person.[1] To Fuchs, self-realization is either meant in the sense of yielding to the process of seeking one's self, or of exclusively psychological realization of the self as not truly "human and Christian self-realization in the full sense of the word."[2] If one merely understands self-realization in a simple sense, one will inevitably absolutize an exclusively psychological self-realization and ignore some other higher values of human reality (such as the interpersonal relation with others and the striving of the self towards the human fulfillment in God). According to Fuchs, the phenomenon of Gesinnung in the human person consists of three aspects: "Responsible self-realization," "Self-realization as radical openness," and "Vertical self-transcendence as self-realization." Let us attempt to explore these three attributes of self-realization.

The first one is the basic and all-inclusive task of each individual person. In simple terms it is a self-acceptance or self-affirmation, which is the opposite of self-denial or self-alienation. It is the task of the entire reality of the self to be actualized through the progressive humanization of the given human existence. This task of "responsible self" ties in the context of our two previous discussions that each human person exists as a responsible creature for the development of both his/her own given existence and the world. This first task of self-realization is subjectively conscious; and for Fuchs it manifests and cooperates with the insights of evaluating reason (such as Bonum hominis est secundum rationem esse) to the extent that "reason has the possibility of arriving at self-understanding, and also at an understanding of individual realities."[3] In other words, responsible self-realization is the process by which the human person consciously and positively accepts his/her own self as a given reality and aligns with the good of the self, for the good of the human person consists in being in accord with reason.

To Fuchs, human reason can help each person understand his/her own self and to discover which of the various possibilities human deeds effectively correspond to the true good of the human person. In understanding this basic task of the human self, Fuchs suggests that "self-realization" is not at all selfish. For it brings home to the human person not the withdrawal into his/her own ego, but rather the positive acceptance of his/her own existence with the understanding of finding the best possibilities to develop the whole person. For Fuchs the whole phenomenon of self-realization begins with this basic responsibility of the self. It is so basic that if one is conscious of self-withdrawal or self-alienation, there will be no self-realization at all in the human person.

The second dynamic attribute of Gesinnung is "self-realization as radical openness." Fuchs uses the term "radical openness" in the broad sense to exclude any arbitrary or indifferent attitudes and decisions of the human person. Namely, the horizontal realization of the self is indispensable for the wholeness of the human person.

The first two areas of this radical openness of the self primarily deals with the external world. The self must be open to the fact that it is indeed in the world (not merely in its own ego), and that this world surrounds the self with many conditions which are both appropriate and inappropriate to the human person. This self-openness, it its worldly facticity, acknowledges the basic fact that the world belongs to the self. The world is not purposeless, but it basically exists for the human person. This world belonging to one self, Fuchs says, is often called "nature" in the simple sense. The ultimate purpose of "radical openness" in its facticity is to allow the given reality of nature to effect the self, and in turn to transform this "nature" into culture. This reciprocal realization of the world and the self is determined by evaluating reason, which interprets the totality of the world and understands the wholeness of the human person. To put it simply, since the self is always in and with the world, the self must not misuse the givenness of the world. Rather, it must appreciate it to the extent that the self should let itself be determined by the world, so much so that the self with its own evaluating reason transforms the world and makes it become human culture. To Fuchs this double or mutual openness is the condition for the horizontal realization of the self with the world. In this given world, with the effort of participating in and transforming what is given to the self, the human person must be open to what is unconditioned in conditioned human reality. In Fuchs' words;

> ... the self must be open to this (the experience of the unconditioned in the midst of the human reality which is essentially conditional), unless it wishes to live in self-alienation rather than in self-realization.[4]

If one denies the basic fact that he/she is actually in and with the world, that person will remain in egocentric selfishness or even worse, in self-alienation and self-contradiction.

With such an understanding of the first two areas of the "radical openness," Fuchs then adds: Openness vis-à-vis the givenness of nature and reason, . . . and vis-avis- the unconditional in the conditional reality of the human person are surpassed by openness vis-à-vis the other."[5] That is to say openness to the other person will enable the self to protect its participation and transformation of the given world. Fuchs defines this third area of radical openness as the outreaching attitude of the human person that God calls in which the self discloses its reverent acknowledgement for the inner most dignity of the other persons. In being radically open to others, Fuchs affirms, the self participates in the love of God for them. It is the love of the self for other persons. Yet, what exactly is this openness to others of the self as its love for them?

Fuchs offers a sufficient analysis of the neighbor-love of the self. He says that the love of the self for others "does not mean this or that good work, but the total openness of the person to another."[6] He even equates this total openness of the self with the giving of the self for others in saying that love of neighbors as such does not induce a person to give this or that, but to give him/herself. Thus, to be open radically to other persons is to love them by way of giving to them the totality of the self. In the simple sense, Fuchs says, we call this phenomenon "of being open to others" the "Christian existence." Thus to be a truly human person is to be open to others and to transcend the self for others. Being open to others enables the self to become a "truly human person" because it is the self-realization in "one of the deepest dimensions of the human self."[7] Inasmuch as one truly is open to others by way of giving to them the total self, he/she will be open to God, for this openness to others is the call of God for each individual. For Fuchs, this final state of self-realization is the vertically "transcending" of the self toward God. This vertical self-transcendence of the human person needs to be explored.

The subjectively responsible self-realization and the horizontally radical self-realization serve as the means for the human person to reach to this final state of vertical self-transcendence. It is the entelechy or the perfection of all the actualization of the human person. This self-transcendence takes place in the inward orientation of the human self, and it is based on the fact that the self has consciously acknowledged the present totality of the human person who is in the world and with others. Fuchs affirms that behind the inmost orientation of the human self there exists something absolutely transcendent from which every human act of transcendence receives its meaning and foundation. In classroom lectures, this was stated as "the reality of being-alone-with-God-along."

Because of this eternal presence of God in the human self as the transcendent ground for the wholeness of the human person, Fuchs concludes that ultimate self-realization does not consist in the selfish fulfillment, but rather in absolute transcendence, which is God. This ultimate self-realization simply means that the human self "goes out from itself in its entirely and transfers itself to God."[8] Fuchs insists that the vertical transcendence of the human self is possible because of our transcendent God who is ever present in us and "imparts himself to us in a particular way in Jesus Christ."[9] True self-realization, according to Fuchs, will be the ultimate realization of the human self in Jesus Christ. The ever availability of Jesus' grace in all human persons (in both Christian believers and non-Christian believers) will enable all to live toward self-transcendence in God. Insofar as one reaches such a realization, one truly comes to the conversion into his/her true self. The conversion from self-alienation into true self-realization is the call of Jesus for each human person qua human person.

However, Fuchs adds that self-realization "will never perfectly succeed before the promise and then definitive gift of the eschatological realization of the self."[10] The process of realization of the human self is not a completion of some intervals of the human life. Rather, it is a perpetual conversion into the ever new person within the assistance of Jesus' grace. The reason for such a continuous conversation, Fuchs suggests is because the human person discovers in him/herself the tendency of the "flesh," which draws him/her into self-alienation. Fuchs makes use of Pauline theology to sustain this point.

In Romans 6-8, Paul convincingly persuades the community of believers of the undeniable fact that we experience ourselves in this world simultaneously as "spirit and flesh." In Fuchs' terms, Paul is speaking of the "self in contradiction," which is the struggle of the human self in its efforts to convert the self with-the-tendency-of-the-flesh into the true self-realization. Paul also exults and professes that God has given each human person the Spirit as the power working against the selfish self. Paul repeatedly insists that the Spirit given to each human person is only provisional and is not yet experienced in its fullness and definitiveness.[11] There remains the case that even with the power of the Spirit the human person still must and should live continuously for the conversion of the selfish self, the idea of homo viator.

Besides the teaching of Paul, Fuchs refers to the instruction of Jesus' Sermon on the Mount (Mt 5–7) to support his understanding of the human self-conversion. Fuchs believes that the first beatitude for the poor synthesizes all the other beatitudes. The truly poor "human person," in spite of being poor or affluent in the eyes of the world, are those who recognize and acknowledge themselves to be poor and weak in their inwardly personal depths. With such an honest recognition, they become open to true riches and true humanity and they are indeed blessed. Inasmuch as one understands that he/she is poor in this sense, Fuchs say, that person remains with the hope of God's promise. Furthermore, what can be said of this honest acknowledgement of the poor self is that the human person will not entrench him/herself behind the selfish interest in searching for the authentic actualization of the self and the world.[12] To Fuchs, this is Jesus' radical mandate for every human person. To be the true self by way of denying the selfish self-limitation or self-alienation.

A summary of Chapter III is in order. The true self-realization of the human person consists in the threefold attributes of the self. It is the willing acceptance of the self, the horizontally radical openness with others, and the vertical transcendence to God via Jesus Christ. The human self realizes itself in reciprocal harmony with the world and with other persons, which ultimately transfers the self to God. God is ever present in the human person and this fact makes the vertical transcendence possible for each human person. This last aspect of self-realization is the most important for Fuchs as he believes it to be the most authentic self of the human person. Self-transcendence is so essential that if there is any perceptive description or ethical judgment about the human person, it must be done from the criterion of this true self-realization. Simply because it manifests the truly human person in its process of continuously transcendental conversion into the ever new person.

Our discussion with Fuchs on self-realization leaves open room for further exploration as to what else in the in most or transcendent human reality can effectively and practically assist the human person, besides God, in continuing such a transcendent conversion into the true self.

NOTES

1. "Morality: Person and Acts," in *Christian Morality*, p. 106.
2. "Self-realization and self-alienation," in *Christian Morality*, p. 143.
3. "Self-realization and self-alienation, in *Christian Morality*, pp. 147–148.
4. "Self-realization and self-alienation," in *Christian Morality*, p. 149, ( ) my rewording.
5. *Ibid*, p. 149.

6. "Moral Theology and Christian Existence, in *Personal Responsibility*, p. 29.
7. "Self-realization and self-alienation in Christian Morality, p. 149.
8. *Christian Morality*, p. 150.
9. *Christian Morality*, p. 150.
10. Ibid.
11. 2 Cor. 1:22, 5:5, Rom. 8:23, and Eph 1:14.
12. *Christian Morality*, p. 153.

Chapter IV

Basic Freedom and Basic Conscience

In this section, we will study Fuchs the meanings of "basic freedom" and "basic conscience." Our discussion can be divided into three subsections: basic freedom and freedom of choice; basic conscience and its role in the objective world and personal orientation; the relationship between basic freedom and basic conscience. In the third subsection, I will attempt to synthesize discussion of Fuchs' view of the moral structure of the human person.

(A) BASIC FREEDOM

Fuchs divides his treatment of "basic freedom" into separate realms: psychological freedom, Christian freedom, and moral freedom. Psychological freedom functions to help the human person makes choices and to pursue aims freely. Christian freedom, mentioned by Saint Paul, is the indwelling capacity of the human person, which is given by the Holy Spirit to keep the mind open to the presence of the Holy Spirit's guidance. Moral freedom allows the human person to achieve a good life through virtuous acts and aims. To Fuchs, the phenomenon of "basic freedom" should be understood in the broader sense than three notions of human freedom presented. In the final analysis, the basic freedom of Fuchs' ethics will encompass all of the above notions of human freedom and more. Our author builds his theology of basic freedom from a basic principle, "as a person, man/woman is free."[1] Fuchs uses this principle in order to discourage attempts at limiting the inquiry into basic freedom, which focus exclusively upon the objects of choice, or abstractly upon the pure possibility of the human person. "Basic freedom" is not the freedom of the ordinary moments of life, which the human person chooses some acts or objects. Neither is it a pure possibility in the human person as if he/she somehow discovered in him/herself the absolute possibility to be or to do whatever he/she wishes to. What exactly is then the meaning of this basic freedom?

"Basic freedom" or "transcendental freedom," as defined by Fuchs, is "the free self-commitment of ourselves as persons," which, in its character of the total activation of the human person. It should be considered more than any particular action or the sum of the acts, for "basic freedom" always underlines the personal acts, "permeates them, and goes beyond them without ever being actually one of them."[2] "Basic freedom" is not the freedom to make a decision to act or to reach the objects of choice, but it is the totally personal act in committing oneself to be a person. To put it more simply, it is the freedom that the human person accepts or denies to realize his/her own self. Since the essential character of basic freedom is either the positive or negative commitment of the human self, it consists ultimately "of the gift or refusal of the self in love to God." This extensive notion of basic freedom toward God is quite evident because God is the ground of human existence, from which one accepts or denies his/her own self. Our author affirms that "the act of basic freedom is the realization of the person as a whole."[3] This illustrates our discussion in Section III of the concept that self-realization consists of the horizontal and vertical actualization of the self with the created world and with God. This would imply that the basic freedom of the human person is a lifetime task of the person.

Basic freedom presupposes the presence of personal realization, in which the human person is conscious of his/her own self as an entity. To Fuchs, in the structure of the human person, the human self-consciousness is on a deeper level than the psychological subconscious. Since basic freedom is based on self-consciousness and self-realization, our author insists that self-realization manifesting itself in openness towards other persons and God "is the true moral commitment of basic freedom of the person."[4] Thus, the basic freedom of Fuchs' ethics must be understood as the freedom of the "*'person as such*,'" and it serves as the means not merely for all concrete and particular actions, but above all for the self-realization.[5] It follows that the human person would never be undecided about the ultimate meaning of its own existence (which is the realization toward other persons and toward the Absolute), for the human person exists with the basic freedom which simply consists either of the negative or positive commitment of the self.[6] Here an objection arises as to whether or not this basic freedom can be intelligible to the personal subject.

Our author believes that "every man/woman has a prior awareness—after more or less reflection—of some essential elements of his/her being," such as "his/her contingency to and total dependence on an absolute; his/her fundamental interpersonal individuality and the corresponding social orientation to others, but above all of his/her own personality, (basic) freedom and responsibility."[7] This simply means that for Fuchs every person by nature is aware of his/her basic freedom, for self-commitment is a free process of the human person, and thus, it can only be done with self-consciousness.[8] However, our author admits that the phenomenon of basic freedom "cannot be explained in psychological categories nor does the free recognition by the personal subject or even a definite theoretical explanation of the deepest self, force this phenomenon onto reflection."[9] The earlier stated reason for this is that basic freedom does not belong to the objective categories, but rather to the transcendental self-consciousness of the human person. Fuchs explains further: in the performance by free choice of a particular moral action, the human person can arrive at an objective knowledge of what he/she is doing either by a conceptual and reflexive or an intuitive manner. Yet in the free activation of the self, the objective knowledge is not possible. In order for the subjective "I" to reflect objectively on the self, in the whole self as a subject, the subjective "I" must remain outside the "I" that is the object of that reflection, so much so that the subjective "I" can act and reflect. Thus Fuchs concludes, "there can be no adequate objective knowledge" of the phenomenon of the basic freedom.[10] That is to say, "self-commitment" (in love for others and for God) is not specifically categorically known, but transcendentally conscious. The human person can only be inwardly aware of his/her own basic freedom in the process of self-realization by being open toward other persons and God. This openness of the human self is either in accepting or refusing other persons and God. In Fuchs' terms, it is the freedom that "we are basically free always and only as loving or sinning, but loving or sinning freely."[11] Yet the readers of Fuchs cannot help but ask how and in what way the human person be conscious of his/her own basic freedom so that he/she can properly activate it and concretely use it in the course of his/her moral life. Our author answers that "the activation of basic freedom is performed not as a distinct act in itself, but in and through an act of free choice," thus we are conscious of basic freedom "in different ways."[12] In other words, we are conscious of our basic freedom in its relation with the freedom of choice. Let us now discuss this relationship between categorical freedom and transcendental freedom.

> We speak of freedom of choice in so far as we are able, in particular acts, to apply ourselves freely to the many possibilities and requirements of life as it unfolds before us in space and time. . . The moral act of free choice can be expressed in an external act or in an inner act of free will. But when we bring to realization, in our free choices. . . , at the same time we engage ourselves as

persons. The personal realization. . . through free choice always means an effort to engage the person as a whole in basic freedom.[13]

From what we read in the above excerpt, it is clear that at the level of personal realization the human person will engage its total self in the mode of basic freedom through the freedom of choices. This is not to say that in every single case there will be an activation of basic freedom by freedom of choice. Our author simply affirms that to some extent there exists a significant interaction between the basic freedom of the human person and the particular moral acts and efforts of that person. This interactive relationship of the categorical freedom with the transcendental freedom can hardly be denied; for if one denies it, there would never be any responsible acts of the human person in his/her spacio-temporal condition. There is no doubt that there exist some categorical acts of the human person which are personal though they do not spring from the true commitment of the whole person. Conversely, there "can be no particular and categorical act of basic freedom," for the human person "can never grasp and engage the totality of his/herself categorically as an object."[14] A question emerges as to when or how basic freedom will be related to freedom or choice? In what follows we will consider Fuchs' three major arguments responding to this question.

First, Fuchs affirms that realization of the self with its basic freedom through freedom of choice, the human person "builds up for him/herself in many specific fields of morality certain fundamental tendencies—virtues and vices."[15] The acts in the freedom of choice, inasmuch as they are freely chosen by the total involvement of the human person in his/her basic freedom, constitute a certain direction or a course of conduct in the areas of morality. This fundamental course of conduct will be good or bad depending upon the "will to follow" of the basic freedom activated toward virtues or vices. Fuchs feels that the basic course of conduct always remains in continuous motion because the human person always exists as the *viator* within the course of his/her life. Only in recognizing the two aspects of human freedom, can we understand the positive and the negative of basic freedom. Through the individual free acts of the freedom of choice, basic freedom can be activated, and be reaffirmed, or turned around into the opposite direction.[16]

Secondly, since basic freedom expresses itself in the freedom of choice which is the result of the "will to follow" which is fundamentally grounded in the human person, our author stresses that in the moral life there exists "an interdependence between basic freedom and freedom of choice."[17] Morality in the true sense can be considered only when human freedom, as basic freedom and freedom of choice, determines actions. This is quite simple and evident. If one acts without the intention or the will to follow the basic freedom, one does not correspond to one's depths of personal self-commitment. Fuchs suggests that these acts are not moral in the true sense, but only by analogy. Conversely, the intention arising from basic freedom, which is on the level of personal consciousness, and not yet manifested in the free acts, and not moral with regard to the nature of *actus perfecte humani*. Thus in order to achieve the truly human acts, basic freedom and freedom of choice must simultaneously be present in order to represent personal self-commitment as a whole in these free acts. In the field of true morality then, there must be an interdependent relationship between the categorical freedom and the transcendental freedom of the human person. To put it more concretely, freedom of choice and basic freedom are so dependent on each other that without each other we do not perform the acts which are truly human.[18]

Finally, because basic freedom and freedom of choice are so dependent upon each other, in the *actus perfecte humani*, Fuchs concludes that they mutually influence each other. This mutual influence can be understood in two senses: in one sense freedom of choice may intensify or diminish the basic intention arising out of basic freedom, in another sense it is the force of the will to follow basic freedom that activates and directs the free acts.[19] In simple terms, the mutual influence of the two aspects of human freedom insists that freedom of choice is the actual practice of the human free acts whereas the basic freedom is the principle of them. The reason for this is because all truly human acts are grounded in the depths of the person with his/her basic freedom.

Fuchs further suggests that the mutual influence of the two can be examined in the phenomenon of the "sign" of the human free acts. The acts of the freedom of choice without any doubt disclose some signs such as good or bad conduct. In the reality of free choice these various signs can discern and disclose what is the "manner of our basic free commitment."[20] Fuchs holds that in the acts that are performed without freedom of choice, hence without the activation of basic freedom, there is no personal commitment to these acts. Fuchs concludes the conjecture based on signs enables us to know the moral certainty and the basic free commitment of our persons, in which the mutual influence of basic freedom and free choice manifests itself concretely through the specific acts of our human lives.

From what we discussed thus far with Fuchs, it is clear that basic freedom exists only in the performance of the free acts which are a result of freedom of choice. These two aspects of human freedom are reciprocally dependent upon each other in the course of moral formation. Hence, basic freedom of the human person continues to actualize itself in the freedom of choice as a fundamental force, and constitutes a particular "moral direction." In other words, basic freedom is the major force in the moral formation or development of the human person, which takes shape in successive "free acts." Our author admits that in the course of moral formation, especially when facing specific situations, human freedom alone as basic freedom and freedom of choice is not sufficient for the human person to achieve "moral goodness." The human person must be open to his/her own personal "subjective conscience," which will provide moral insights to make moral decisions. In the effort of achieving "moral goodness" there exists a relation or cooperation of basic freedom and personal conscience. As our author suggests, "we are speaking of (basic) freedom and conscience, one is unthinkable without the other;"[21] let us now move to our discussion of the personal conscience in the fields of the "true morality" of the human person.

(B) CONSCIENCE

Common understanding of the human conscience is derived from two viewpoints on the function of conscience in the areas of morality. First, the function of conscience from the static view, which applies to the behavioral norms of actual individual instances. Second, from the dynamic standpoint of view, conscience is seen to interpret given situations hermeneutically and to search for the certainty of fundamental values and moral insights.[22] Fuchs suggests that the phenomenon of conscience has various aspects. Conscience can be regarded as the authority of the personal ego which strictly governs the conduct of life. Conscience can be seen as being bound to and cooperating with practical reason in making moral judgments with regard to practical reason. Conscience can be experienced as religious to the extent that the human person is conscious of the ultimate significance of his/her being toward the Absolute to whom he/she commits his/her own person. Conscience can be seen as the means for the improvement of the personal "ethical maturity" in the course of moral conduct. The first two aspects of conscience Fuchs calls the object-orientation of the conscience. The latter two Fuchs names the subject-orientation of the conscience.[23] In what follows we will study with Fuchs the primary subject-orientation and the secondary object-orientation of the phenomenon of the human conscience. It would be helpful to begin with the subject-orientation.

Fuchs suggests that in order to understand the true essence of the conscience-phenomenon we must return to the phenomenon of "human self-consciousness," which fundamentally is the realization of the human self. At the deepest level of consciousness the human person "is aware of him/herself . . . as an existence bound by obligations, a moral being. This is the deepest core of the conscience as personal subject."[24] Elsewhere, Fuchs analyzes the conscientious phenomenon by saying "in developing one's conscience toward a position (a moral conduct) and a judgment one gains a glimpse of the innermost essence of conscience."[25] That is to say, at the deepest level of consciousness the human person experiences his/her own conscience and must exercise it in the course of moral conduct in order to comprehend the essence of his/her own conscience. Our author states that this conscientious experience is the basic phenomenon of the human person. It is the subjective orientation of the human person, which presupposes self-conscious realization, and the presence of the personal basic freedom. Since Fuchs' understanding of conscience focuses on the level of personal exercise and practice, one cannot help but ask what is the aim or the purpose of this basic conscience in the human person? Fuchs responds that the subjective orientation of the person can be expressed in various ways: it can be in the personal concerns of being bound by obligations; in the personal responsibility for one's self-realization; in personal faithfulness to the true insights of conscience; in the personal experience of the requirement to remain receptive to the given world and to be open to other persons. All of these various aspects of personal orientation, Fuchs continues, concern the "morality of the personal subject." Our author affirms that they indeed are the genuine imperative made by the basic conscience in its fundamental subject-orientation.[26] Thus, the primary interest of basic conscience is the concern of the moral goodness of the personal subject. This is the sin and the purpose of the subjective conscience of the human person, according to Fuchs.

Since the primary interest of the subject-orientation focuses on personal "moral goodness," the function of basic conscience is to enable the human person not merely to act in a morally correct way, but above all to act "according to what the conscience recognizes as being right."[27] That is to say, the act of basic conscience is the involvement of the whole person in its personal responsibility of acting according to the appropriate call or the challenge of worldly situations. With such an understanding of basic conscience, Fuchs then affirms that "moral goodness is the personal fidelity to the conscience's judgment."[28] Granted this analysis of the basic conscience, an objection here emerges as to what if there exists the "erring conscience" in the subject-orientation. To this problem of erring conscience Fuchs offers two responses. First, if the errors occur in the sphere of moral action (such as applying norms or making decisions), those errors are not concerned with personal goodness, but with the correctness of moral judgments in the conscience, namely, with object-orientation. Secondly, if errors take place when the conscience's erroneous judgments are complied with the primary function of conscience, these errors have nothing to do with moral norms but with the personal subject-orientation; namely, moral goodness. In either case, the matter of "morality" or "immorality," Fuchs expressly affirms, does not consider the fact that the human person accepts or rejects the "morally correct act" and the "morally good conduct;" but above it all it is concerned with the phenomenon that the human person take necessary pains and efforts but fails to achieve such a correct act and a good conduct.[29]

It is clear that the basic conscience of Fuchs' ethics is the responsible conscience. Since it is responsible, it is personal and unique in each human person. Thus only when the human person remains faithful to his/her own conscience for certain moral conduct (either good or bad depending upon his/her aims at virtues or vices), will true morality of the human person exist. Our author admits that "the personal subject always fulfills itself only when it emerges from itself and steps into the categorical object of the world and becomes responsibly active there, conscience has to be object- orientated."[30] Basic conscience must be exercised in concrete decisions and acts of the object-orientation for moral conduct, else there would never be human acts based on the conscience's insights. Let us now move to the discussion of the objective aspect of the human conscience.

Even though the object-orientation of the conscience is considered as secondary, Fuchs affirms that this secondary aspect of conscience is also important "for the conscience-phenomenon as a whole."[31] The study of the object-orientated conscience is the analysis of how conscience provides "orientation for a correct human conduct," which ultimately concerns itself with the material content of the functioning conscience. Our author offers four arguments concerning the basic conscience's function of providing moral judgments: first, the evaluative and normative function of conscience in all cultures and traditions; secondly in dealing with a specific situation the moral person remains with his/her conscience alone; thirdly in applying the universal norms for a specific situation the conscience must first interpret them; and finally the compromise of the conscience in dealing with the norms which are incompatible with a concrete situation. Let us consider each in particular.

First, Fuchs holds that any individual person is not an "isolated island within his/her object-orientated conscience." Each person exists in a certain society which has a certain culture and tradition. Whatever one considers in his/her life to be humanly and morally justifiable has been determined by the longstanding tradition and culture to which he/she belongs. While moral convictions and practical reasons are presumably different in different cultures, Fuchs affirms that they are for the most part the result of the rational insight of the subjective orientation of conscience. Basic conscience is always evaluative and normative in any culture and tradition. The reason Fuchs holds such a universal character of the normative and evaluative conscience in pluralistic cultures is because he firmly believes that the human being "is fundamentally able to get insights of the practical reason," and that the hope of seeking the practically certain moral truths will never abandoned in any cultures.[32] Thus to Fuchs the moral judgments always presuppose the evaluative and normative function of the basic conscience so much so that the moral decisions and moral acts arising out of the conscience's insights are personally responsible.

Secondly, in making moral judgments for a specific situation the moral person always remains with and only deals with his/her own basic conscience. Moral judgments being made by the basic conscience in a particular situation are judgments which exclusively belong to the personal subject who must responsibly reach some decision about the given situation. At this point our author explains what he means. Analytically speaking, the access to the moral insights of basic conscience (i.e., the personal interpretation of the situation), the judgments made by conscience for moral correctness (ie., the judgment of how or which manner to act), and the personal moral decision (i.e., the decision to act) "all take place simultaneously."[33] From the logical order there may be a succession among these three acts, but from the viewpoint of time there is neither a preceding nor subsequent situation among them. Fuchs concludes, at the moment the basic conscience reaches an actual decision, there involves not only a particular action, but also the whole person who is the moral subject. Thus, in any specific situations there always remains the demand of personal involvement with one's entire being, which ultimately is not concerned with objective norms but with the "personal basic conscience" alone.[34] Even in some specific situation in which moral judgment is influenced by moral experience, guidance, and norms; moral judgment, nevertheless, remains unique and specific judgment which has never been made before by the personal subject in this particular situation. Again, in the specific situation the judgment in the conscience for concrete moral correctness is unique and should be concerned with the subjective conscience alone.[35]

Thirdly, in assessing the existing universal norms and applying them to a specific situation, Fuchs says that there remains always the fact that moral judgment must be made by the personal subject. The moral person must interpret the norms and the situation in order to come to a truly responsible "moral judgment."[36] There is no doubt that moral norms of correct conduct and some other normative social authorities can enable the moral person to reach the moral judgment for the concrete situation. Fuchs affirms they are yet merely assistance for the process of morally correct decisions which ultimately must be made by the basic conscience. Since the application of universal norms for a concrete situation is ultimately concerned with personal moral judgment, the matter cannot be reduced to the content of objective norms. Neither can it ignore the appropriate call and the moral challenge arising from the concrete situation. Above all it must consider the personal responsibility for the moral person, not the demanding content of the universal norms, which confronts the situation, interprets it, and makes decision to act in it.[37]

Finally, the difficulty of applying the norms to a concrete situation entails the concern of the compromise of the conscience in facing some incompatible values of the universal norms with regard to the situation. The term "compromise," Fuchs says, is not used in the actual meaning of "moral binding."[38] It merely refers to the solution to which the basic conscience would prefer when being challenged by the incompatibility of norms with the situation. Some moralists, including our author, experience that "norms regarding correct conduct within the world always reflect the earthly and limited good/ values possessed by human beings."[39] Since they are limited by the fact that they are the products of human thoughts, they may be incompatible in some concrete and confined situation. In such a problematic case, the solution for the consideration of the qualities and values should be given. Fuchs stresses that it must be a compromise of the conscience alone.[40] In other words, it is up to the conscience itself to choose which level of the hierarchical values of norms are utilized in making a moral decision.

It is clear from our study of Fuchs' understanding of the phenomenon of the human conscience that the function of the conscience is not merely to transmit or to provide the mode of right behavior. Rather it activates and makes manifest personal responsibility as the wholeness of the moral person in the field of morality. The human conscience is not passive before demanding norms, but rather active within the objective world in its personal insightful interpretation and subjective discretion. The active and responsible character of conscience has been clearly demonstrated in Fuchs' analysis of the subject-orientated conscience concerning primarily with moral goodness, and of the object-orientated conscience dealing concretely with moral correctness. The mutual influence and the interactive dependence between these transcendental and categorical orientations consist primarily in the responsible role of personal conscience. Because the acts of conscience, in either a concrete behavior or an intentional conduct, remain always personally responsible, they require the existence of personal freedom, which can ultimately be considered as the moral acts of the moral person. This is why Fuchs has to posit the personal basic freedom in his perceptive analysis of the conscience-phenomenon. Thus, with regard to Fuchs' thoughts of the true morality concerned with personal moral goodness, basic freedom and basic conscience are the two aspects of the one entity which is called the human person. Basic freedom and personal conscience are so related that in the absence of one or the other there would never at all exist a true act of the moral person.

Let us now make a few remarks with regard to the relation of the basic freedom and the basic conscience. In what follows we will summarize Fuchs' notions of "basic freedom and personal conscience" by way of constructively analyzing three pragmatic considerations: (1) whether the fundamental direction being constituted by basic freedom and freedom of choice is discernable by the moral person him/herself, (2) whether the subjective conscience of Fuchs' ethics is situational, (3) whether the human person of Fuchs' writings is capable of achieving a genre of ethical life.

(C) THE RELATIONSHIP OF "BASIC FREEDOM" AND "BASIC CONSCIENCE"

1. Is the fundamental direction discernable?

In the subsection on basic freedom, we have arrived at the conclusion that the knowledge of the fundamental direction can be achieved by means of conjecture based on signs of the course of moral conduct. The readers of Fuchs cannot help but state that those signs, perceptively speaking, disclose to other persons not to the moral person him/herself. Granted on puts great effort in arguing that those signs must naturally disclose to the moral person him/herself, for it is the moral person who creates those signs in his/her moral conduct. Such an argument will not avoid the difficulty of the transcendental epoche in which the personal subject will never reach the objective knowledge of him/herself. This difficulty of the transcendental epoche Fuchs has addressed at least twice in Section IV. Signs, ultimately speaking, always disclose to and for other persons.

If they are always for other persons, an inevitable question emerges as to whether the moral person him/herself truly discerns his/her own fundamental direction of morality. If one tries to find the answer for this question merely in Fuchs' theological treatment of basic freedom, one would end up with a hopeless and disappointing situation. For our author has clearly stated that the basic free self-commitment, i.e. the fundamental direction cannot be other than conscious. It cannot be objective and reflexive but mere transcendental and unreflective in the inner core of the personal subject.[41] If this were the case, the readers of Fuchs would unhesitatingly conclude that the moral person of Fuchs' writings does not quite surely know but can only guess or hope about his/her own fundamental direction.

If one pays retrospective attention to Fuchs' analysis of human conscientious phenomena, one will see that basic freedom is nothing other than the responsible freedom to activate and to exercise the genuine imperative or the demand of the conscience. The subject-orientated conscience basically demands the moral person to pursue personal moral goodness, which can only be achieved on the ground of the "will to follow" of basic freedom. The readers of Fuchs may perceive that Fuchs is too optimistic in his perception of the human person to the extent that Fuchs persuasively convinces every human being of the undeniable fact that he/she is basically free and his/her own conscience fundamentally demands a morally good conduct. Indeed, Fuchs' positive and optimistic view of the human person has the person's ontological ground in the image of God. This grounding may have been affected, but not destroyed by original sin. In a sense, Fuchs' optimistic view brings hope and encouragement for any person who wishes to pursue an ethical life within his/her own human capacity and condition. It is the hope that each human person by nature is responsibly free and consciously called toward the moral goodness. If the basic call of the conscience is to motivate the personal subject, to move toward moral goodness, and if the basic attitude of the moral person is free with such a genuine conscientious imperative, there remains a basic phenomenon that the human person either responds to or refuses that basic conscientious invitation. The human person by nature cannot be indifferently passive or arbitrarily undecided about his/her own moral person. In making this basic decision of fundamental direction, the human person must be conscious of such a basic decision as the human person is basically free in doing so. It follows that the human person must discern the direction of morality into which he/she invests the totality of his/her person. Thus, it is clear that the fundamental direction is discernable in conscience by the moral person him/herself. Insofar as the moral person discerns his/her own fundamental direction, the remaining challenge will be the phenomena of the conscience in being responsibly active in the objective world. Fuchs suggests that conscience must be realized and exercised so the moral person may gain his/her own conscience in the course of moral conduct. Conscience in Fuchs' writings is not the conscience to perform an act but to be developed along with its personal subjective realization. This is an admirable point of Fuchs' ethics on the human conscience for it stresses the sublime notion that human ethics, in every sense of the term, should be the ethics not of the human acts but of the personally responsible "moral life."

2. Is the subjective conscience truly situational?

If the fundamental direction is consciously discernable, the role of the conscience must be active in the personal subject and in the objective world. The created world surrounding the human person is indubitable in its character of being *deja-toujours-donne*. It always exists for the human person. From a phenomenological perception, the objective would must be distinguished from the human person who in his/her own intentionally reaches out to grasp some objective knowledge of the world and of his/her own human objective condition. It follows that there exists a gap between the world and the human person. Fuchs covers this gap by depositing the humanizing process in his treatment of human self-realization. The human person of Fuchs' writing is placed in the objective world where it is responsibly active for the development of the world and of the personal self. As Fuchs has clearly admitted, the personal subject fulfills itself only when it steps into the categorical objects of the world.[42] Now if the purpose of being in the world is to fulfill the whole person of oneself, all of the acting behaviors and conducting direction of the human person will not primarily aim at performing the deeds for concrete situations, but above all at the improved development of the whole person. It follows that all deeds and conducts arising from the genuine imperative of the subjective conscience are not particularly situational but rather personally eternal.[43] In a sense the objection to Fuchs' notion of human conscience as being too situationalist and subjectivistic is legitimate to the extent that all personal moral judgments must remain faithful to the rational insights of the personal conscience. Fuchs has handled this weak part of his writings quite well. In his analysis of the human conscience, Fuchs has interpolated his conviction of the fundamental human ability to acquire insights of practical reason; his belief of the human basic freedom for realizing the self; his persuasion of he creatively interpreting role of the conscience with regard to the norms and situations; and his articulation of human consciousness of the distinction between moral goodness and moral correctness. With all of these personal qualities, the human person of Fuchs' writings is still not blinded and subjectivistic, while remaining faithful to the conscience's insights alone for the moral judgments. If the subjective conscience of Fuchs' writings were cooperating merely with the freedom of choice, it would be subjectively situational; this is not the case. The human conscience of Fuchs' ethics, as we have assiduously studied, presupposes the basic freedom and indeed cooperates with it in the formation of the moral goodness and moral correctness. It is clear that the subjective conscience is not situational, but personally responsible to the objective world and the human self in the process of both categorical and transcendental orientations.

3. Which ethics?

We have seen that the human person is able to discern a fundamental direction, and that the human conscience is not selfishly situational but responsibly moral. The remainder of our concern for this Section IV is the type of ethics of which the human person of Fuchs' writings is practically capable. Without any doubt, the human person of Fuchs' description is the adult; who commits him/herself as a person; who is capable of acquiring rational insights of practical reason for the conscience to interpret the moral perspectives; and who articulates his/her basic freedom to set forth a fundamental direction for morality. The readers of Fuchs cannot help but say that such a description of a mature person does not need a prescription of the types and levels of ethics that exist. Fuchs circumvents this objection of his readers by reminding that due to the obstacle of the concupiscent ego the process of self-realization will not completely succeed until the eschatological self is being fully actualized.[44] By arguing the possibility that the improvement of the human person cannot be ignored or excluded when moral judgment is reached at the higher level of moral maturity.[45] The human person of Fuchs' writings is always in need of the pursuit of an ethical life. Readers of Fuchs may wonder which ethics are these? Fuchs never defines his own ethics and indeed he never wishes to do so, interestingly though, Fuchs is well known as a distinguished theologian of the moral subject.[46] He even spends time in numerous articles to deal with the question of whether or not there is a specific Christian ethics.[47]

In a simple view, the readers of Fuchs can say that the ethics for the human person of Fuchs' description must basically be a humanistic ethics or at least a personally responsible ethics due to the very fact that the human person of Fuchs' writings is so responsible in both moral behavior and moral conduct. This perception is quite legitimate in light of what we have been studying thus far. The ethics of Fuchs is not so simple. It is quite complicated due to the complexity of the phenomenon of the human person. We will see this when we come to the second part of the paper. Be that as it may, let us begin our study of Fuchs' ethics with his suggestion that "I believe that within the sphere of Christian ethics the focus should be placed, above all, on the primacy of moral goodness as opposed to moral correctness in the world, and that proportionate focus should be placed on the primacy of the conscience's subject-orientation as compared with its object-orientation."[48] Let us now move to the second part of the paper.

NOTES

1. Basic Freedom and Morality, in *Human Values and Christian Morality*, pp. 92–93.
2. Ibid. p. 96.
3. Ibid. p. 96.
4. Ibid. p. 95.

5. The Phenomenon of Conscience: Subject-Orientation and Object-Orientation, in *Christian Morality*, p. 120.

6. *Basic Freedom and Morality*, p. 97.

7. Human, Humanist and Christian Morality, in *Human Values and Christian Morality*, p. 145. Parenthesis is added.

8. *Basic Freedom and Morality*, p. 105.

9. *The Phenomenon of Conscience*, p. 121.

10. *Basic Freedom and Morality*, p. 105. To support this point Fuchs quotes from the Council of Trent (DS 1534 f.) which affirmed that no one has certain knowledge of the state of grace. Fuchs believes the state of grace the Council referred to is the basic free love of the human person for God. Notice this difficulty of the adequate human knowledge of one's basic freedom. We shall return to this point in due time.

11. Ibid., p. 97. We have seen in Section III that Fuchs perceives love as being the realization of the self to other persons and to God. Now Fuchs introduces his notion of "sin" which is the opposite of "love." "Sin" in this context is the direction in which the human person with his/her basic freedom chooses to turn away from others and from God into the selfish ego. Notice "sin" to Fuchs' ethics implies the basic freedom of the sinner. We shall have occasion to return to Fuchs' treatment of "sin" in the second part of the paper.

12. Ibid.

13. Ibid. p. 98.

14. Ibid. This point is related to the impossibility of the objective knowledge of the human self which we have classified in the previous paragraphs. Here Fuchs explains that as soon as the human self as the personal subject grasps at itself as an object, the subjective self that is acting is no longer found within the self confronting itself as an object. In other words, in trying to grasp itself as an object, the human self always remains as the subject in order to do so. This is the transcendental epoch (or epoche) of the human self in its own phenomenological perception. (For reference see Edmund Husserl, *Cartesian Meditation*, Fifth Meditation).

15. Ibid., p. 101.

16. Ibid.

17. Ibid., p. 102.

18. Ibid., pp. 102–103.

19. Ibid., p. 104.

20. Ibid., p. 107.

21. The Question Addressed to Conscience, in *Personal Responsibility*, p. 217. Parenthesis is added.

22. Ibid., pp. 219–220.

23. The Phenomenon of Conscience, pp. 118–123.

24. Ibid., p. 124.

25. The Question Addressed to Conscience, pp. 220–221. Parenthesis is added. Notice Fuchs does not define "conscience" but merely offers his perceptive analysis of the phenomenon of conscience. Let us keep this in mind in order to understand why Fuchs firmly holds that human conscience must be personal and unique in dealing with the given situations.

26. Ibid., p. 125.
27. Ibid.
28. Ibid., p. 127.
29. Ibid., pp. 125–127.
30. Ibid., p. 128.
31. Ibid., p. 128.
32. Ibid., pp. 128–129. By "practical reason" Fuchs simply means the moral insights with which one makes a moral judgment. Here is Fuchs' example of how he understands the moral judgment being based on the "practical reason:" "whether one as a member of a certain cultural society considers that to take loving care of an aged person up till his very last breath satisfies the demands of piety, or whether in another culture one considers that it is not permissible according to the rules of piety to allow an aged person on his own account as well as on that of others, to suffer the burdens of old age, is in both cases understood as being explicitly based on practical reason."
33. Ibid.
34. Ibid. To support this point, Fuchs quotes from *Gaudium et Spes*, no. 16 and explains that "the moral subject is quite alone with its conscientious decision, theologically speaking, with and before God."
35. Ibid., p. 130.
36. Ibid., p. 131.
37. Ibid., pp. 130–131.
38. We shall return to the discussion of moral compromise in due time. It is the moral concern in which the moral person should and must minimize the premoral "evils" and maximize the moral "good" in achieving a moral end. It is also the moral concern of the principle of double effects in which the moral person must act according to the proportionate or commensurate reason.
39. Ibid., p. 132.
40. Ibid.
41. *Basic Freedom and Morality*, p. 105.
42. *The Phenomenon of Conscience*, p. 125.
43. By the adjective "eternal" in this context, I do not mean a long period of physical movement. I simply mean the lifetime task of moral person which begins when one truly commits oneself as a responsible person and it continues until the eschatological self is being fully actualized.
44. *Basic Freedom and Morality*, p. 96.
45. *The Phenomenon of Conscience*, p. 123.
46. We shall discuss this complicated issue of Fuchs' writings in the conclusion section of the paper. In my opinion, the simple reason for Fuchs to avoid to indicate the specific title for his own ethics, it is because he does not want to reduce his ethics to the categorical system which somehow would disqualify or deny the transcendental freedom and the subjective conscience of the human person. Further, if there is any adjective which can be indicative to the ethics of Fuchs, I think such an adjective must

be the dynamics in order to include and retain the mutability of the human being which we have diligently studied with Fuchs in Section II of the paper.

47. Cf. Is there a Distinctively Christian Morality? Is There a Normative Non-Christian Morality and Christian Morality: Biblical Orientation and Human Evaluation.

48. *The Phenomenon of Conscience*, p. 132.

Chapter V

God's Salvation in Jesus Christ is the Genuine Morality

God's incarnation in Jesus Christ leads to the only morality that is in accord with the human person on the basis of his creatively being. God, the creative and continuing origin and fundamental active source, has come forth from himself and has entered into the other whom he willed: a first incarnation of God. Thereby, "having become man," he has also entered into the morality which alone can allow the human person to become truly human: because the creator Spirit of God is in it. In order that men may live for him—i.e. in a human manner, not sinfully—he became man in Jesus Christ and imparted a share in his Spirit.[1]

This excerpt serves to answer the question of which genre of ethics has been the concern of Fuchs' writings in the preceding section. The author insists that the incarnation of God in Jesus leads to the only one morality. It is the truly human morality which is the salvation and redemption of God in his Son. The foundation of this morality is based first on the order evidently found in creation, and finally on God. In what follows there will be a discussion on the ground Fuchs' humane ethics and the role of God in the inner worldly behavior of the human person.

The Declaration of Religious Liberty affirmed that the highest norm for human conduct is the "divine law," which is eternal and universal, and which God orders to govern the world and human beings (no. 3). Even though the Declaration was not concerned with a positively 'given' divine law but simply with human morality, Fuchs observes that the formula "divine law," however, did give many Christian believers the impression that "our ethics in reality is a positively divine decree."[2] The phrase "divine law" in the context of the Declaration, Fuchs believes, is the reminiscence of the "eternal law" in Augustine's and Aquinas' theology. Divine law or eternal law simply expresses that "every ordering of created reality, including the moral order of the human person, is present in the eternal reality" of the omniscient God. The moral order for Fuchs includes: the most general moral insights, the moral norms, the moral divergences in various cultures, and even the concrete ethical judgments being made in the individual situations.[3] To say that the moral order is grounded in the eternal law of God is the same as to say that God allows human beings to share in his law. This human participation in the theonomy of omniscient God is not something incidental, but rather it is intended by God in creation and thereby quite personal to the human person. The author affirms that it is by means of conscience that God makes us become sharers in his eternal law.[4] It follows that the ethical natural law or humane morality is the divine law itself even though it exists only in the participatory form. Since the explicit attribute of the ethical natural law is the human participation of theonomy, Fuchs stresses that human morality must be "identical with what it is to be human . . ."[5] In other words, the true morality must insist on genuine humanity which is the human self-realization per se for it is the human participation, not anything else, in the eternal theonomy.[6] Granted the human person, by participation in the wisdom of God, can attain a moral insight that is correspond to God's wisdom and eternal law, an inevitable objection then emerges as to whether or not the human person can attain the fullness of eternal theonomy. Fuchs gives a negative answer to this question and amidst that this is the limit of true morality. This is why the formula "divine law" cannot be understood as a positively written decree handed down to humankind for their moral conduct. It is also why the demand of the moral order correspond to the divine wisdom in some particular cases, Fuchs concedes, seems to be too much to ask of the human person.[7]

In acknowledging the limit of his theology of the true morality, Fuchs renders another source for its foundation, namely, God's incarnation in Jesus Christ. God has created the human person and then enters into this human reality. In simple terms, God's incarnation is something new to the human person. This something new that is not human joins the human person and even penetrates the human freedom itself. Divine incarnation is the creator Spirit of God who, by becoming human, enables the human person to become truly human. It is obvious that in his theology of incarnation Fuchs treats the human person with a special perception that the human person is not merely a created image of God, and not solely a participatory partner of God's wisdom, but it is a being who receives the creative Spirit of God. To put it more simply, the human person of Fuchs' theology is an "incarnate spirit" whom God creates and affects with His spirit in Jesus Christ for the moral conduct toward the fulfillment of true humanity.[8] Fuchs concludes that the redemption through incarnate Jesus Christ means above all "the liberation and redemption of the human being . . . from his state of being closed in upon himself, making him in his inmost being open to God and to men, to all that is true and good, and thus to the renewed and better discovery of his own self...."[9]

Thus the true ethics consists primarily of God's salvation in Jesus and it must be humane in the best sense of the term due to the simple fact that God's salvation for humankind has taken place in the form of human reality. The author takes the suggestion of Council Fathers in *Optatam Totius* to support his point in saying that "... moral theology should not proclaim first of all human morality, but the salvific action of God."[10] This primary task of true ethics, Fuchs affirms, is quite clear in Paul's message that genuine "belonging to Christ" is what matters above all for any moral attitude and conduct.[11] If the true ethics of Fuchs' writings is salvation morality in its human attribute, a question emerges as to how God intervenes in the moral field of the human person.

Fuchs brackets off the formula "commanding God" and "ruling God" from his ethical theology for they like the phrase "divine law" have created a false impression that God gives humankind a written decree and directly involves in the inner worldly behavior of the human person. The author acknowledges that although all human discourse about God needs to be analogously anthropomorphic, yet a hyperanthropomorphic articulation applied to God is completely unacceptable.[12] If God were commanding and ruling in the categorical behavior of humankind, God would not take seriously the human world as a gift of participation in His omniscient being, and there follows that the categorical commanding on the part of God would make divine incarnation become superfluous. Further, if one represents the human being as "the remote-controlled agent of a divine law,"[13] one will lack the most humane attribute of the human being that is the incarnation of God. Humanity in the proper sense of the term expressly denotes God's incarnation for it is God who created a participation of the human person in His own divine reality.[14] Thus, the author suggests that one should not "... directly involve the creator God further in the process of finding knowledge of the divine wisdom which has, in fact, become incarnate—i.e., in finding knowledge of the morality of the created human being."[15] For one cannot and should not present God as the one who appears on the scene or morality with his specific inner worldly demands and rights alongside with the created human being. This is not to say that God does not count as the ontologically transcendent ground for all things and for human morality in the sense of 'radical agnosticism.' It is rather, Fuchs explicitly contends, the genuine "... acknowledgement of God as God and the humble acknowledgement of human morality as merely human participation in God's wisdom on the basis of his incarnation through creation."[16] It follows that God in his transcendent lordship of creation does not act "by constantly intervening in the course of human history," but he rather "has set human beings free" and made them become responsible for the development of their own selves and of the world.[17] Thus, a humane morality should be understood as the incarnate divine wisdom to the extent that it is the human person itself who interprets and discovers how human conduct is to be valued in the light of the human participatory divine wisdom. If human morality is the participatory wisdom of God within the responsible judgment and interpretation of the human person, the ethics of Fuchs' writings will be faced with a concrete question as to how far moral truths have their salvific significance, or to put it better, what it is the truth of this human morality.

As having been discussed in previous sections, Fuchs' ethics distinguishes personal goodness from personal badness and moral rightness from moral wrongness. Indeed Fuchs has rendered this neat distinction from the tradition called 'proportionalism' and placed it in the context of his theology of salvific incarnation.[18] The moral rightness/goodness distinction leads Fuchs to the distinction between "moral truths" and "truths of salvation." The author suggests that the formula "moral truths are truths of salvation" cannot be properly understood without constructive distinctions of the question of the right behavior from the question of salvation.[19] As having said above, salvation concerns the wholeness of the human person and thereby it is identical to the personal moral goodness.[20] That is to say, the question of personal morality consists primarily of the truth of salvation. While "moral truths" concerns merely with the rightness of categorical behaviors and thereby they are morally true not in themselves, but in analogous sense. One should not misunderstand that personal morality is individual morality. It is rather that the personal morality deals with moral goodness and problems of the individual person. The author states that in human worldly activity the moral rightness of the action and the moral goodness of the person both should coincide together in the reality of salvation, namely, they should be the effect and sign of salvation. This is the salvific significance of Fuchs' human morality. Only understanding in this way, can one speak of moral truth as the truth of salvation and can one count humane morality as the reality of salvation without confusing the properly salvific element, i.e., personal moral goodness, with moral rightness in the ensemble of human salvific response to divine efficacious love.[21]

Since Fuchs appoints divine law and salvation to be the foundation for his humane morality, he then determines that there is one true law for human morality, viz, the law of Christ. Indeed it is the person of Christ himself is the law of human morality.[22] According to Pauline theology in Colossians, Christ is not only *Verbum* of God but also the archetype in whom and through whom all things were created. Thus Christ is ". . . the measure of life for all."[23] In concrete terms, the person of Christ is the pattern of and for human life. Yet "life" in this Christo-centric context does not means merely existing as a human person, but it means above all "living as Christ."[24] Through incarnation Christ gives his own life to each human person as one's possession so that it is by means of Christ' Spirit each human person has capacity to "will and to love" according the person of Christ, who is the personal archetype for true morality. Thus the law of Christ, Fuchs affirms, should be understood so that the person of Christ is the ontological measure of the human life, and the Holy Spirit is the effective activity of the Christ in each individual person for one's striving toward the fullness of Christ himself.[25] There is no doubt that the law of Christ must include the formulated commands found in the gospel such as the command to love one's God and neighbor. To Fuchs, those outwardly formulated commands are the secondary elements of the law of Christ. The primary element of *lex Christi* is the grace of Christ given within each human person. The secondary elements of lex Christi serve to help the human person not misunderstand the grace of Christ and thereby not to interpret it in the selfishly egoistical manner.[26] Thus the law of Christ is ". . . .the inner grace of the Spirit of Christ, which powerfully leads the individual to form in himself the image of Christ, and to form it in that full measure to which the Lord calls the individual."[27]

In summary, for Fuchs there is only one humane morality which is salvation morality. It has its firm ground in divine law of creation, in God's incarnation in Jesus Christ, and thereby in the law of Christ. This true ethics has its most explicit character that is the human participation in God's wisdom, which ultimately consists in the life, and the person of Christ himself. In simple terms, the human ethics of Fuchs is an ethics for Christ-effected human persons. The human person of Fuchs' genuine morality is an incarnate spirit, who has been allowed to share in God's wisdom, and who has been given the Spirit of God by Jesus Christ. Again the readers of Fuchs find his positive perception of human being, which lead Fuchs to investigate a humane ethics that is possible for all human beings. As seen above, Fuchs insists that the redemption of Christ means primarily the liberation of the human self from he alienated state to the true realization. "This self-realization of the person as such and as a whole is also the free realization of the inmost free reality of person, hence also of his 'belonging to Christ'."[28] If the ultimate message of Fuchs' ethics is the consideration of genuine humanity, his ethics then must be possible and available to all human persons regardless of the fact that the human person has a thematic (*Wissen*) or nothematic (*Bewusstsein*) knowledge of Christ.[29] For this ethics simply requires the moral person to achieve an aretaic perfection that is to become the true self in its form of humane fullness which is the sign of belonging to Christ. This is why Fuchs affirms that the grace of Christ within each human person's conscience will teach one, better than an ethics of values and a code of rules can do, to understand the meaning of one's own life whose archetype is the person of Christ himself.[30] Fuchs' humane ethics based on the law of Christ suggests a further investigation on his understanding of law or at least his perception of moral absoluteness. Thus, the next section will focus on Fuchs' concept of natural moral law and of its binding force in norms with regard to the human conscientious interpretation and judgment in finding the moral solutions correspond to the ensemble of human realities.

NOTES

1. "God's Incarnation in a Human Morality," in *Christian Morality*, p. 50.

2. Ibid., p. 51. Fuchs also believes that some Council fathers without explicit reflection understood divine law as a positively divine decree which in itself is directly accessible to human mind.

3. Ibid.

4. Ibid., p. 52. The Council fathers in the quoted encyclical explicitly said that "It is through his conscience that man sees and recognizes the demands of the divine law" (no. 3). Fuchs interprets conscience in this context as ". . . the possibility inherent in the human person of understanding himself as a moral being and of attempting to bring the manifold ethical problems and questions to a valid solution." This is the reason why Fuchs holds that all moral judgments being made by the human person must remain faithful to the moral insights of one's own conscience. See Section IV above.

5. Ibid.

6. Ibid., p. 53. Notice the character of true morality for Fuchs must be human. If it is human, it must be individual and unique in the dynamic and responsible conscience of each moral person. This is why Fuchs prefers not to discuss the content of true morality, for the inquiry of the ethical content deals merely with the personal rightness but not with the personal goodness. Thus the author just sets the ground of the true morality in the human character with the purpose of affirming that this true morality is possible to all human beings.

7. Ibid., pp. 53–54.

8. Even though Fuchs never uses the phrase "incarnate spirit" to refer to the human person, yet his treatment of human nature and his theology of incarnation explicitly stress that the human person has its ontological ground in God's being, and that God's incarnation effectively penetrates the human person and its freedom. Thus this present writer deliberately employs the phrase "incarnate spirit" to denote Fuchs specific understanding of the human being, viz, it is human not in the secular and common sense, but in the sense of an incarnated humanity.

9. Ibid., p. 61. Notice in this context of ethical subject, Fuchs' theology of incarnation does not emphasize deeply the mystery of Jesus Christ becoming human flesh. This is understandable for the author does not mean to treat the subject matter of

Christology. Yet, it is interesting to see that Fuchs renders his theology of incarnation to qualify the enormity of the human character of the true morality.

10. "Vatica II: Salvation, Morality, Behavior," in *Christian Morality*, pp. 20–21. See also *Optatam Totius* (No. 16).

11. "Early Christianity in Search of Morality: 1 Cor 7," in *Christian Morality*, pp. 95–98.

12. "God's Incarnation in a Human Morality," in *Christian Morality*, p. 61.

13. "Our Image of God and Inner Worldly Behavior," in *Christian Morality*, p. 47. Fuchs suggests that the proper interpretation of the human being described in the first book of Old Testament should be that human being is ". . . a dialoging and cooperating partner whose existence is distinct from the rest of created world."

14. "God's Incarnation in a Human Morality," in *Christian Morality*, p. 57.

15. Ibid.

16. Ibid.

17. "Our Image of God and Inner Worldly Behavior," in *Christian Morality*, p. 47. By emphasizing God as the transcendent and not as categorical lord of human behavior, Fuchs wants to maintain the enormous role of "personal responsibility" in his understanding of humane ethics. Besides this reason, if this present writer is not mistaken, Fuchs prefers to begin his understanding of the absoluteness of morality not with God but with "natural law" which is the expression of the ensemble of human being. As Fuchs puts it himself, "Like Kant, I hold that God is the point of arrival, not the point of departure of ethical reflection" ("Come Kant ritengo che Dio sia piuttosto il punto di arrivo, e non il punto di partenza, della riflessione etica"). "Discussione: Natura Cultura Assolutezza," in *Morale e coscienza storica: In dialogo con Josef Fuchs*, p. 60.

18. See, e.g., Bernard Hoose, *Proportionalism: The American Debate and its European Roots* (Georgetown: Georgetown University Press, 1987), pp. 41–63. Due to the limit of this book, the present writer prefers not to do a study of the chronological development of the distinction between moral goodness and moral rightness. A brief review would be sufficient. According to Hoose, this neat distinction had first appeared in G.E. Moore's *Ethics* (London, 1958), in which Moore warned that the moral praise or blame, in moral enterprise, is often confused with the question of what is right or wrong. Hoose shows that Shuller picked up this distinction from British philosophy and developed it further in the context of Christian morality. In his article on "proportionalism" Schuller emphasized that any ethical norms concerning concrete behaviors can only be the application of more universal norm which necessarily covers the matters of salvation and moral goodness (B. Schuller, ur Problematik allegemein verbindlicher ethischer Grundsatze", Theologie und Philosophie 45 (1970): 4). Hoose proves that Schuller's insights have influenced the writings of Fuchs and Janssens on the theme of moral goodness and salvation (B. Hoose, *Proportionalism*, p. 45). However, if this present writer is not mistaken, Fuchs' understanding of this distinction is quite different from that of his moralist colleagues in that the moral correctness is not the moral person-subject as such, but rather it is the humanized development of the world-object. As Fuchs puts it himself, "L insieme delle sue decisioni e attivita personali nel mondo non sono il soggetto stesso, ma sono attivi sviluppi

personali del mondo-oggetto, che continuamente si succedono e variano." "Storicita e norma morale," p. 16. This point will be discussed again in due time.

19. "Moral Truths—Truths of Salvation?," in *Christian Ethics*, p. 62.

20. Ibid., p. 50. By all means, human response in the form of personal moral goodness is not the totality of divine salvation. It is merely a necessary part on the human person whereas divine grace that is the efficacious love of God is another part of the salvific reality.

21. Ibid., p. 53.

22. "The Law of Christ," in *Human Values*, p. 78.

23. Ibid., p. 79.

24. Ibid.

25. Ibid., pp. 84–87.

26. Ibid., p. 86.

27. Ibid., p. 91. At first glance it seems that Fuchs contradicts himself in that on the one hand Fuchs holds that God has set human being free for the whole duration of history, and on the other hand Fuchs' lex Christi affirms that it is Christ who leads human being progressively toward the fullness of Christ Himself. This seeming problem will be solved if one pays a careful look at Fuchs' theology of incarnation which expressly states that the grace of Christ means nothing other than the within capacity of each human person which Christ gives and enables each person to become truly human, namely, become humane in one's ethical self.

28. "Early Christianity in Search of Morality: 1 Cor 7," in *Christian Morality*, p. 95.

29. "Is There a Normative Non-Christian Morality?," in *Personal Responsibility*, p. 72. See also, "Is There a Distinctively Christian Morality?," in *Personal Responsibility*, pp. 59–60. Fuchs borrows this concept of "thematic" and "athematic" knowledge of God from the tradition called transcendental theology, among which Karl Rahner's theology of unanimous Christians was the famous one. This fascinating point of Fuchs' theology yet leaves open to the important question as to whether or not there must be a distinctively Christian morality. Fuchs gives a negative answer to this question with many reasons. The basic one is that, as having seen in Fuchs' theology of incarnation, God's call to salvation is universal for all human persons, to which human person in turn should and must respond by realizing and developing their own given beings toward human perfection, viz, toward genuine humanity. Thus the totality of salvation, namely, God's call and human response, consists primarily of the genuine humanity, that is, the redeemed humanity from the state of both "alienated selfhood" and "being wayward from God." Further if one prefers to investigate concretely the content of Christian morality, Fuchs contends that one will ultimately find nothing other the human elements as such in that morality, regardless the indubitable fact that such a morality has been arising from a Christian community. Fuchs uses the phrase "Christian intentionality" to describe the fundamental attitude and decision of Christian believers, who have accepted God's love in Christ, died with Christ, and are risen with Him in faith and sacrament. The author suggests, if one abstracts the transcendental aspect of this Christian intentionality, one will find that "Christian morality" in its categorical conduct is basically a "humane orientation,"

and that Christian intentionality, though being an element of Christian morality, does not determine its content (*Personal Responsibility*), p. 57). The simple reason for this, it is because the moral consciousness of the Christian community is basically derived from a "human" understanding. This is not to say that there is no specific character of Christian morality, but simply to affirm that "humaneness" is its essential attribute. This precise fact leads the author to affirm that the meeting point of Christian and non-Christian moralities is "human morality" in the best sense of the term (Ibid., p. 79). This is why, if this present writer is not mistaken, the proper interpretation of Fuchs' ethics must be the understanding of his ethics as "humane morality." The present writer is also fully aware that at some point Fuchs admits that human morality is a analogous participation in the lex Christi (Ibid., p. 78), which would seem to amount to say that Christian morality is a genus in which all species of human morality is participating. Fuchs has covered this weak part of his ethical argument by encompassing the Christianum and the humanum in his understanding of Christian intentionality (Ibid., p. 63). That is to say, the ultimate element and concern for Christian morality cannot escape the requirement to e humane from the aretaic effort of the Christian believers. Besides contending that the content of Christian morality is humane and not distinctively Christian, Fuchs also polemically affirms that the non-Christian morality, especially human morality, can arrive at some insightful solutions and answers correspond to the moral rightness of human behavior. In other words, Fuchs firmly believes that Christian and non-Christian believers have the same task of always seeking to "individuate the concrete humanum" for moral conduct. This task for Christians and non-Christians, Fuchs stresses, was so dear to the Council fathers of Gaudium et Spes n. 33 (Ibid., p. 78).

30. "The Law of Christ," in *Human Values*, p. 81.

Chapter VI

Natural Law and Moral Norms

When addressing the subject matter of morality and rights, one inevitably speaks of the realities that have "binding force" with regard to the human person and community. "Natural law" has been one of those "binding forces" in moral literatures. The term "natural law" is being used in both the areas of law and rights and of morality, Fuchs notices, has created several misunderstandings that "nature" as such can offer to human persons norms and laws of correct behavior. To avoid this naturalistic fallacy, one must acknowledge that "in effect, the creature-nature speaks to us. But it says to us only what it is and how it functions of itself."[1] There is no doubt that the terms "law" and "norms" are analogous in their linguistic applications, which should be admitted in order to understand their "binding force" without disregarding the significant role of the subject-person who is the responsible author for the realization of the true self and of the humanized world. In what follows there will be an attempt to study Fuchs' understanding of "natural law" and his perception of "moral norms" for correct behavior of the human person. The reflection in this section will cover the historical nature of norms for moral correctness with regard to the historicity of human being.

The concept of "absoluteness," besides its theological sense of referring to God, can be discussed in a "non-theological" sense such as in law and in ethics. Fuchs affirms that moral "absoluteness" has its meaning not in particular orders of morality and rights, but in the true meaning of the human person as such. The reason for this is because:

> God does not give positive rights and duties to man; rather, man is the image of God and participates therefore in God's providence. Humanity therefore must try to discover by itself an order of rights and morality for man and society in this world. The binding force of the order of rights and morality, found in this

way, is absolute because it is founded in the reality of man himself, created by God and redeemed in Jesus Christ.²

From this excerpt, it is clear that in human being there is found an absolutely binding moral order. This fundamental "moral order" is called "natural law," which, however, in its moral sense is not a written moral code of norms. Rather it is an absolute moral obligation of the human person to find the inner worldly way of living by which one expresses the true meaning of one's life. To put it more concretely, moral natural law is the self-obligation of each human person, which requires one to realize one's human nature to the fullness of true humanity. Needless to say, "human nature" in this context is not an abstractly metaphysical concept, but rather it expresses the ensemble of the human realities which constitute the human person here and now. If the *absolutum* of moral natural law is a demand of an ethical level from the human person, and thereby has its ground not in the created nature but in the human person, there follows that moral natural law in itself is "man himself insofar as he can understand and formulate normative moral propositions and judgments in a right way."³ In other words, natural law is the responsible effort of the human person in projecting and discovering "an order of human self-realization" because the human person is an historical and moral being and therefore the human "given nature must be more and more humanized" by the human person itself. It follows that moral natural law in itself is not metaphysically evident but rather moral certitude to the extent that it is the human person itself who finds this natural law in the structure of one's historical being and hermeneutically interprets it with one's own right judgment of reason (*recta ratio*). Fuchs insists that there are two ways of speaking about natural law. Philosophically, natural law expresses the phenomenon in which the human person experiences one's self as an historical being which is in need of self-developing toward the fullness of one's own historicity. While theologically, it expresses the salvific reality in which God has set the human person free and responsible for one's constantly striving for "a right and better understanding" of one's being, and correspondingly pursuing a process of humane realization.⁴

Since the human person is constitutively historical, the aretaic endeavor of discovering the natural law must also be basically historical, namely, it must be creative in itself. In interpreting and judging the ensemble of human historical being, the human person discovers the correctness of human doings and the right realization of the world, from which one "draws the greater part of moral norms."⁵ This process Fuchs calls "hermeneutical reading of concrete reality," from the result of which norms of natural moral law (*legge morale naturale*) justify and individuate themselves. In other words, "natural law" by the creative effort of human *recta ratio* will successively manifest itself in the positive law or in the moral norms of correctness. Fuchs puts it more forcefully, "natural law itself needs to be positively recognized and stated in society," so that its binding force can be efficient and its uncertainties in the form of laws or norms can be re-evaluated and ended.[6] Only in this way, Fuchs insists, can one have a proper appreciation of positive laws and norms without suppressing the significance of natural law in human nature which demands a perpetual possibility of interpreting and re-evaluating laws and norms, corresponding to the here and now moments of human historicity. Granted this is the case, an objection here emerges as to how the hermeneutical reading of laws and moral norms is to be established. The author admits that "the question is difficult and today still debated."[7] If "hermeneutical reading" of moral norms in it practical operation is the significant role of the subject-person, the establishment of "hermeneutical reading" must be based on the responsibly conscientious self of the human person. For without the human self, the *absolutum* of "natural law" and the "binding force" of moral norms would be meaningless and superficial. Thus Fuchs insists that "It is man, created/called to act reasonably and responsibly, who has to interpret, evaluate and judge under the moral aspect the further realization of the given nature."[8] It follows that there is no criterion for the "hermeneutical reading" other than the human responsible self itself. For, logically speaking, if the fundamentally obligatory interpretation of creature-nature (*natura-creatura*) fell under a criterion other than the subject-person, such an interpretation would become superfluous because the criterion itself says sufficiently what the human person should do for one's ethical life, which would be amount to say that there is no need of the human personal responsibility and freedom. This is not the case simply because the primary task of the human person is not to fulfill the demand of a criterion or a norm, but to seek the way to true self-realization. It is clear that "natural law" and moral norms mean nothing other than the genuine humanity itself, viz, *humanum*.[9] If moral norms are an historical result of the human hermeneutical interpretation of the creature-nature, there arises concrete questions as to what it is the nature of moral norms and how they do function in the realm of human correct behavior and of the world's right realization. In order to reflect on the nature and the function of moral norms, Fuchs suggests as following:

> Returning now to the problem of moral norms, it becomes possible to focalize certain very important points. Man-subject is an historical and moral being, which realizes itself in the realization of the creature-nature, which presents also itself a continuous history of its own. This creature-nature, besides, is never grasped in a purely "objective" manner, but is found to be constantly already

interpreted and evaluated. Only considerating man in this perspective will it be possible to perceive and formulate moral norms; only thus can one understand how moral norms are to be understood.[10]

Since the understanding of moral norms depends primarily and entirely upon the historicity of the human person and its fundamental interpretation of the creature-nature, a brief review of human historicity in this context of the argument would be helpful. According to Fuchs, the human person always perceives one's self unthematically as a moral being with a basic task to live not only the present moments but also the past and the future, through out the course of which the human person is always the same subject, but lives in a history in time and space that encompasses all capriciousness. The basic task in this historical process facilitates the human person to seek solutions which are better corresponding and more suitable for the successive moments of life, by means of which the human person values the ensemble of concrete realities and then acts correspondingly.[11] This is the historicity of the human person. As Fuchs puts it himself, "This is an historical process, without end, and proper because it is so, [which] constitutes man as a moral being with a task . . ."[12] It has to do with "the subject-person as well as the human realization of the world-object (*natura-creatura*)," the former of which is called "moral goodness" while the latter is termed "moral correctness."[13]

Fuchs affirms that the concept of moral goodness remains basically the same through out the history of moral theology, while the notion of moral correctness does not do so. The simple reason is this: "The reality of the world . . . undergoes profound transformation; scientific readings of the reality of the world-object . . . remains largely hypothetical and can eventually change; human interpretation of fact and of historical evolutions are not necessarily always the same; evaluations which follow from them are also themselves multiple and depend in large measure on the vision of the world (*Weltanschauung*) which the individual more or less freely assumes."[14] If evaluations of the world-object depend primarily on the multiplicity of human interpreting, by all means they cannot be static as a completely objective solution for the historical human self-development and for the continuous realization of the world. In this sense, Fuchs concludes that "The judgment on the correctness of human dong is not of its own and in itself a moral judgment or a moral norm,"[15] for such a judgment or evaluation in fact responds primarily and merely to the concern of which realization of reality is humanly appropriate or inappropriate.

To say that moral judgments and evaluations are multiple in responding to the continuous concern of right realization of human subject-object world, it is the same to say that they are indeed participating in the human historicity, within which they have their own history. This implies that there is a continuity as well as a discontinuity of norms of moral correctness. That is to say, the hermeneutical reading of norms correspond to the human correct doing and to the right development of the world, does not only seek to understand the content of norms, but must take into account their historical character, so much so that the hermeneutical reading in itself can be valid. Because of this, Fuchs states that ". . . not all norms can be materially the same and be valid for all circumstances and for all time."[16] Thus, it is indispensable that the human hermeneutical reading of norms must evaluate "the inherited normative of the past."[17] This perception of the nature of norms would be more accepted if one considers the human consciousness of each generation in the human history. Fuchs believes that each generation has its own way of interpreting and evaluating the human reality and the world-object. This is to say, that ". . . there is no doubt that men of future generation will change with the passing time, they change the way of understanding, interpreting, and evaluating themselves."[18]

If norms of moral correctness are based on the creative interpretation of each human generation, there emerges a doubt on the "objectivity" of norms to the extent that norms are merely formulated by the subjective effort of the human person. Fuchs expressly affirms that there must be the objectivity of norms, yet it ". . . is an intrinsic exigency, but never completely realized: it is necessary to have always new attempts to conduct norms of acceptance until now to a greater, always more complete 'objectivity'."[19] The continuously exegetical need for the objectivity of norms is quite understandable in light of the significant role of the historical being human person. For the human person cannot create a moral judgment that is entirely separated from one's own understanding of the ensemble of one's human realities.

It is clear, therefore, that norms in their objectivity, coming from a "cognitive-evaluative-judging process," are determined not only by the appropriate development of the world-object, but also by the true realization of the human subject-person. Hence, in order for norms to be truly objective, they must say what they indeed demand within an indispensable reference to such a double aspect object-subject reality, viz, to the world and the human person. The demand or the binding force of norms suggest their practical functions for the perceiving subject-person in the course of moral conduct.

There is no doubt that the human person either as individual or as a society live well with norms of moral correctness. But this is not to say that human historicity has reached its complete historical transformation. Indeed, the historical human person still goes on as a subject to further realization, in the course of which norms express the moral truth or truths of the reality of the subject-person and of the world. Such norms Fuchs calls norms of moral correctness. He affirms that they "... are most useful in order to orient a concrete moral judgment, but nothing more than very useful, since in their abstract formulations they cannot refer formally and exactly to the truth of concrete reality of here and now."[20] In other words, the functions of norms are merely an assistance for the moral correctness of the human person and for the right development of the world. If norms are merely an aid to the subject-object reality, there follows that their application cannot be all together univocal, but rather it must be analogous. In the simple terms, even though norms have their truth/objectivity, but their application is not absolute and unlimited.[21] For the application of norms must take into account an indispensable "hermeneutical reading" of the concrete "here and now" of the ensemble of the human person. This understanding of Fuchs' on the function of norms is quite consistent with his perception of the historical character of norms.

If the function of norms is not absolute for all time and thereby merely analogical in providing the solution for the concrete here and now reality, it implies the need for evaluation of the norms themselves. There are some general cases in which norms must be re-evaluated. First, some norms in the past, by means of an understanding radically diverse from that of today, were formulated for concrete realities which are profoundly different from those of here and now existing. Second, some norms of the same considered realities which did not take into account of an understanding that is new and was never consciously discovered in the past. Finally, some norms have been inadequately formulated and thereby do not offer sufficient response to the concrete realities here and now.[22] When facing a doubt of "the effective capacity of offering valid solutions" of norms, Fuchs expressly suggests that "... there is imposed a critical-hermeneutical reading of norm itself."[23] In other words, the value of norms for Fuchs must be continuously interpreted and judged by the responsible subject-person for norms in their proper sense are nothing other than the expression of what is suitable and correspond to the ensemble of the human person. Because of this, the author concludes that norms of "correct realization of the world-object" can be called moral only when they demand the "personal goodness" of the subject-person itself.[24]

In summary, Fuchs' concept of natural law and moral norms is understood in reference to the human historical being that is still going on in its historical transformation. The subject-person of Fuchs' writings always perceives itself as a moral being in the sense that the subject-person always experiences within itself the fundamentally moral obligation of historically self-realizing to the authenticity of every single moments of its own human ensemble. This basic moral self-responsibility, in Fuchs' term, is "natural law," from which the human person, within one's own historically hermeneutical reading, discovers suitable solutions and values for one's own present existing ensemble of reality. From such a lively and creative role of the human responsible self, there arrives some norms for the true realization of the subject-person and the right development of the world-object. These norms Fuchs calls norms of moral correctness, insofar as they can be founded as the expressions of the correct realization of the "world-object," which includes the worldly right development and the personal correct doing. Yet these norms can be called moral only when they express and demand the personal goodness of the subject-person as such. If norms in their historical character seek to gather the values of the ensemble of human realities, and thereby express the moral goodness of the subject-person, an inevitable objection emerges as to what it is the relationship of normative values with the "good" of the moral person. This objection suggests a further reflection on the values of norms and the "moral good" of the agent who involves oneself in the process of developing one's own self and the world, which will be the topic of the next section.

NOTES

1. "In effetti, la natura-creatura ci parla. Ma essa ci dice solamente che cosa essa è e come funziona da se stessa." "Storicitá e norma morale," p. 25.

2. "Faith, Ethics and Law," in *Christian Ethics*, p. 118.

3. Ibid., p. 120.

4. Ibid., pp. 119–120. These two expressions of natural law are in moral sense, whereas its simple sense, denoting the created order of God's creation, which we have already covered in Section I above. However, the present writer believes that Fuchs is not so much interesting in the simple sense of "natural law" for it easily creates the false impression of naturalistic fallacy. By stressing the created order of creation, Fuchs only means to affirm that original sin did not destroy or corrupt completely the human nature and the world. That is to say, "created nature" for Fuchs is still redeemable on the basis of the indubitable salvific fact of incarnated Christ.

5. "Della correttezza dell'agire umano tratta la maggior parte delle norme morali." "Storicitá e norma morale," p. 22.

6. "Faith, Ethics and Law," p. 125.

7. "La questione è difficile e ancor oggi dibattuta." "Storicitia" e norma morale," p. 25.

8. "È l'uomo, creato/chiamato ad agire ragionevolmente e responsabilmente, che deve interpretare, valutare e guidicare sotto l 'aspetto morale l'ulteriore realizzazione della natura data." Ibid., p. 26.

9. This present writer believes that Fuchs would acknowledge this identical affirmation of "natural law" with "*humanum*," for Fuchs explicitly says that "Today many theologians and philosophers, including myself, prefer to speak of the humanum and of "human rights" instead of "natural law." "Faith, Ethics and Law," p. 114.

10. "Ritornando ora al problema delle norme morali, ci diventa possibile focalizzare alcuni punti scottanti. L'uomo-soggetto è un essere storico e morale, che si realizza nella realizzazione di una natura-creatura, la quale presenta essa pure una sua storia continua. Questa natura-creatura, inoltre, non è mai colta in una maniera puramente << oggettiva >>, ma si trova ad essere constantemente gia interpretata e valutata. Solo considerando l'uomo in questa prospettiva sará possibile percepire e formulare delle norme morali; solo così si può capire come devono essere comprese le norme morali." "Storicitia" e norma morale," p. 21.

11. "Discussione: Natura Storia Moralita," in *Morale e coscienza storica*, p. 45.

12. Ibid., p. 46. "Questo è un processo storico, senza fine, e proprio perché è così, constituisce l'uomo come essere morale, con un compito . . ." This perception of Fuchs on the human "without end" historicity is quite coherent with his understanding of human self-realization. To Fuchs "self-realization" will not succeed until the moment of the eschatological realization of the self. See "Self-realization and self-alienation," in *Christian Morality*, p. 150.

13. "Storicitá e norma morale," p. 21.

14. Ibid., pp. 22–23. "Le realtá del mondo . . . subiscono profonde trasformazioni; le letture scientifiche delle realtá del mondo-oggetto . . . rimangono largamente ipotetiche e possono eventualmente cambiare; le interpretazioni umane dei fatti e delle evoluzioni storiche non sono necessariamente sempre le stesse; le valutazioni in larga misura dalla visione del mondo *Weltanschauung*) che il singolo più o meno liberamente assume."

15. Ibid., p. 23. "Un giudizio sulla correttezza dell'agire umano non è, di per sé e in se stesso, un giudizio << morale >> o una norma <<morale>>."

16. Ibid. ". . . non tutte le norme possono essere materialmente le stesse e valere per tutte le circostanze e per tutti I tempi."

17. Ibid., p. 29.

18. Ibid., p. 17. ". . . non c'è dubbio che anche gli uomini delle generazioni future cambieranno, con l'andare del tempo, il modo di comprendersi, di interpretare, di valutare."

19. Ibid., p. 32. " . . . è un'esigenza intrinseca, mai completamente realizzata: c'è bisogno di sempre nouvi tentative per condurre le norme finora acetate ad una maggiore, sempre più compiuta <<oggettivita>>." It should be noted that the term "objectivity" in this context of Fuchs' argument is different from that of commonly being understood. Usually, a norm is called objective only when such a norm is proposed by a competent authority or it is accepted commonly by a society. Fuchs' conviction of a historical development of norms leads him to maintain that the objectivity must be exegetical along with the historicity of the human person.

20. Ibid., p. 34. ". . . sono utilissime per orientare un giudizio morale concreto, ma niente più che utilissime, dal momento che nella loro formulazione astratta non possono riferirsi formalmente ed esattamente alla verità della realtà concreta, dell' *hic et nunc*."

21. Fuchs holds this point also with regard to human rights and law (*Recht*). See "Faith, Ethics and Law," p. 124.

22. "Storicitá e norma morale," pp. 34–35.

23. Ibid., p. 35. "... si impone una lettura critico-ermeneutica della norma stessa."

24. Ibid., p. 23. Elsewhere Fuchs holds this same viewpoint in concerning the absoluteness of norms. The author explicitly states, "The absoluteness of a norm depends more upon the objectivity of its relationship to reality than upon its universality." "The Absoluteness of Behavioral Moral Norms," p. 138. It should be noticed that when Fuchs uses the formula "the correct realization of the world-object," he refers to both the right development of and the world and the correct doing of the human person. This is how Fuchs distinguishes the subject-person from the personal activities in the world-object: "L'insieme delle sue decisioni e attivita pesonali nel mondo non son oil soggetto stesso, ma sono attivi sviluppi personali del mondo-oggetto, che continuamente si succedono e variano. Il soggetto come tale vi è presente come loro sorgente; egli stesso inoltre si sviluppa nello sviluppare il mond-oggetto (se stesso incluso)." "Storicitá...," p. 16.

Chapter VII

Human Acts and Their Values

The reflection in this section will fall into three parts: the nature of human acts and their limitations; the values of human acts and moral knowledge; and the incarnation of personal morality in human acts as the only true moral act of the human person.

> In fact, morality in the strict sense belongs to the person, to the self and to his internal attitudes; only the free person can be moral or immoral . . .—the self with its free attitudes. . . The acts are not morally good or evil in the strict sense of the word, but rather right or wrong insofar as they can be judged suited or unsuited to the reality of the human person and his world, or tending to lead to or away from the good of the human individual, of mankind, of humanity.[1]

From this excerpt of Fuchs', it is clear that the human acts are different from the subject-person to the extent that they are not moral in the strict sense of the term because only the subject-person can be moral. However, Fuchs adds that "The morality of the acts as such is, rather, morality in an analogous sense—because it is measured not by the attitudes of the person but by the fittingness of the acts to the good of the person and of his world."[2] That is to say, one should understand human acts in terms of their relationship to the moral attitudes of the subject-person. Since human acts in their values of rightness or wrongness are related to the personal moral attitudes of goodness or badness, it follows that the values of the acts and the personal attitudes must coincide in the subject-person itself, for it is the subject-person who is the source of its own attitudes and values. However, the author admits that "... unfortunately, this is not and will not always be the case in a being with such great limitations as the human person. Personal moral goodness is always possible. Not so the identification of the rightness of conduct in our world, and the realization of such rightness."³ In other words, the personal moral attitude always seeks to realize itself in acts, but it is not always easy due to the limitations of the human being, without the account of which the significance of the values of human acts would be meaningless. Thus, in order to proceed the reflection on the nature of human acts, it would be helpful to analyze these limitations which, as Fuchs affirms, condition the acts of the subject-person. Fuchs understands these limitations of human being as followed:

> The reality with which we have to work . . . and to develop contains limitations on human possibility. These limitations can derive from the fact of creaturely or historical finitude, and would therefore also exist in a world without sin . . . They may also derive ultimately . . . from the "sin of the world;" as they in fact do, on account of the concupiscence of mankind, on account of the objectification of the "sin of the world" in society . . . and because of weakness due to the concupiscence of the acting subject.⁴

"Historical finitude" and "original sin-conditioned" creation are two of the basic kinds of the limitations for human possibility of acting rightly. The former is quite obvious in the natural history of humankind and of the world. The latter needs to be clarified in this context of the discussion. Needless to say, this perception of Fuchs' on the "sin of the world" is not an affirmation of the total corruption by "original sin" of the created nature. The term "sin" in the phrase "the sin of the world," Fuchs uses in relation to "original sin" in the sense that "original sin is the primordial situation of guilt in which our freedom and its history, from the very beginning, are situated and embedded."⁵ In the simple terms, "the sin of the world" is the sin-conditioned reality by which the "original sin" did affect the subject-person and the world. Fuchs divides the results of this embedded "original sin" into three areas: the concupiscence and egoism of humankind, the objectification of "sin" in human society, and the weakness of the acting subject-person. The first one is the "sin-conditioned" character of the world and of humankind, and the second one is the "required and adapted" systems or institutions of human society emerging from the first, while the third is the individual concupiscence which is the weakness of the acting subject-person. Fuchs holds that these three "sin-conditioned" characters situate human acts, and that they are relevant to the formulation of objective moral norms.⁶ They are disvalues and premoral evils, which list human acts in the sense that they negatively affect the well-being of humankind. Fuchs defines them as "illness, death, underdevelopment, depression, cultural deprivation . . . anything in the earthly, human areas that in one way or another is opposed to the well-being and development of the human being."⁷

Accordingly, there arises the problem of human morally right acts with regard to the limitations of human beings, viz, the human person is quite limited in one's actions in the inner worldly behavior. The author puts it more explicitly, "man . . . cannot realize premoral human goods or values without realizing premoral human evils at the same time in the same act."[8] In other words, there is always the coexistence of the premoral values and disvalues in the acts of the subject-person. Yet, it is necessary to notice that these premoral values and disvalues do not refer immediately to the moral attitudes of the person as such, for they merely belong to the category of the well-being of the subject-person, viz, to the rightness or wrongness of the human acts.[9] The premoral values or disvalues do not offer the moral knowledge of the personal morality, but of the right or wrong acts. An objection then emerges as to how an act of the human person can be known as right or wrong.

The author answers that it can be known by means of considering the coexistence of premoral goods and evils of the act, and evaluating which of the two are so prevalent in the act itself with regard to the most explicit and pressing character of certain values in the concrete situation of the act. This is quite simple in the case of all premoral goods being preoccupied through out the process of the act, but what if there involves the realization of the premoral evils in the act itself. The author asserts that "the realization of premoral evils could be justified only because of the prevalence of the premoral goods as opposed to premoral evils."[10] Granted one can introduce premoral evils in one's act on the basis of the prevalence of the premoral goods, a difficulty arises here concerning how far one can do so with consideration of the effect of premoral evils upon the acting person. Fuchs clearly states that "Human beings who are affected by such evils are not . . . morally evil. But a morally good person has to avoid, as far as possible, premoral evils; his purpose is rather to crate premoral goods and values for the well-being of human beings."[11] So in facing the coexistence of premoral goods/evils, the acting person is required not only to reduce the involvement of the premoral evils but also to create the premoral goods. Yet, creating the premoral goods is more important because it serves the well-being of the acting person and the development of the world. This notion of "creating the premoral goods" will be clearer if one considers the case in which the acting person must sacrifice one particular value in favor another. In this case, Fuchs contends that the solution cannot be the simultaneous realization of the morally rightness and wrongness, but only "the morally right, which, however, contains both nonmoral right (good/value) and nonmoral wrong (evil/disvalue)."[12] That is to say, "creating the premoral good" is the rightness of human acts even though in its implementation contain disvalues or premoral evils. This is how Fuchs understands the values of human acts. They are the "overcoming of the limitations of human possibility," and the "creating further right realization of human beings" in the inner worldly behavior. In achieving these values one gains moral knowledge of what is right and good. Such a knowledge is a moral achievement for "it exists in a single subject who both knows and strives, and [it] is dependent on a greater or lesser personal willingness to pursue what is right and good."[13] Human acts of the inner worldly realization enable the acting person to discover the rightness and the good for one's own self and the world.

Moral knowledge of human acts as rightness or wrongness can be more intelligible if one considers the details and the context of human acts. As the author himself suggests, "Morality, in the true (not transferred or analogous) sense is expressible only by a human action . . . which originates in the deliberate and free decision of a human person. An action of this kind can be performed only with the intention of the agent."[14] If one speaks of the deliberate intention of the acting person, one must take into account its three elements: action, circumstance, and purpose of the moral agent. These three elements, Fuchs says, are premoral in themselves and their actualization in a human act are not a combination of three human actions. Thus a moral judgment must be formed "under a simultaneous consideration of the three elements (action, circumstance, purpose),"[15] for the realization of these three elements belongs to a single human action. This point leads the author to hold that (values of norms) cannot be moral "unless circumstances and intention are taken into account."[16] It is simply because ". . . the values exist, but in the concrete not all values, not in every time, not in every moment of the individual life are [they] actual. They can be perish or acquire actuality."[17]

With this understanding of values of human acts, Fuchs then concludes that no premoral good, except "the divine and the personal moral good," is an absolute good for human beings, and likewise no premoral evil is an absolute evil that has to be avoided absolutely.[18] The personal moral good is absolute and "moral evils" are those "which, if freely realized, make the human being (as a whole) morally bad."[19] If moral good and moral evil are absolute which the acting person can discover in one's acts, there follows that moral attitudes are the fundamental principles of acts to the extent that moral good or moral evil facilitates and requires the acting person to perform the corresponding acts. Fuchs is not so much interested in analyzing the meaning of moral evils. Because moral evils, even though being evils in themselves, do not indicate which human concrete acts that are not morally right. They merely refer to "the moral quality of the person, his moral goodness, and are in this sense 'intrinsically evil.'"[20] This is why the author reminds that "it is not so urgent that it requires the 'absolute,' 'universal,' '*intrinsece malum*' character that applies to the realm of good/evil personal morality."[21] Namely, there is no need of negatively universal norms for moral evils simply because moral evils do not indicate any human acts that are intrinsically evil. There is no doubt that there can be the case of "moral badness" such as when one's act is motivated not by the well-being of humankind but by one's own egotism. But in such a case a moral judgment, for Fuchs, can be only that the acting person is not morally good. In other words, moral evils, as the realization of premoral evils within the deliberate effort of the acting person, signify not the intrinsic evils as such but the negative quality of personal moral good.

If moral evils merely signify the negative of personal goodness and thereby do not offer positive moral knowledge of personal morality, the discussion of truly human acts remains interest in the "moral goodness" that for Fuchs is an absolute good for personal morality. With regard to the relation of moral attitude and moral acts, the author reminds that "To affirm the distinction between moral goodness of the person and the moral rightness of the action . . . does not signify that the two distinct realities are separate and without intrinsic relationship with one another."[22] Fuchs expresses the intrinsic relation of these two realities as follows:

> Personal morality (goodness) is concerned with moral rightness of conduct only to the extent that personal goodness makes us internally and sincerely disposed to seek to identify—together with others and with moral authorities—what is right behavior in the various fields and situations of human morality, and to behave in accordance with what has thus been found and has therefore become an interior light and guide for the moral decision (which is always interior) of the personal human being.[23]

If moral goodness is an absolute good, whose "moral role" is to enable the interior subject-person to seek to identify the moral rightness and to act correspondingly, it is necessarily to state that true moral acts of the human person consist primarily not of "acting right" but of *"incarnating the good"* of the personal morality into the inner worldly well-being of human beings themselves. In other words, just as only the subject-person can be moral in the strict sense of the word, only the acts of incarnating the interior "personal goodness" into the morally right conduct can be moral, so to say. In addition, if humane morality is concerned primarily with personal goodness, it must do so, therefore, by considering the realization of the personal goodness as the true moral acts of the human person. It is necessarily to stress that the "incarnating personal good" is not a passive process in the interior subject-person, for it is sought by the acting person itself to be identified with what is right behavior in the ensemble of human reality. The author expresses this point in a different way, "In fact, the correctness of the human action demands to be accepted and assumed, in human action, from the personal morality, that is fro the moral goodness of the subject-person."[24] Thus it is clear that only "incarnating or realizing" the personal good is truly moral while "acting rightly" is moral in analogous sense. If one objectifies this point by emphasizing the causality of the "acting right" upon the moral person, Fuchs unhesitatingly responds that "It proved difficult, however, to perceive the rightness of conduct is not directly related to the personal morality of the human person, i.e., to his moral goodness . . . Only slowly did it come to be understood that right or wrong behavior, purely as such does not affect personal morality."[25] Therefore, the intrinsic relationship of moral goodness with moral rightness, strictly speaking, is not bilateral but only unilateral association of the personal good being incarnated into the moral rightness, and not vice versa. Thus Fuchs concludes that "when a personal human being is morally good and, therefore, a man of the grace of salvation, he accordingly takes care that his particular self-manifestation in its effect in the world can be integrated into the entirely of this whole world, i.e., into the world of the human person and of humanity; it is in this that rightness of behavior in this world consists."[26] When the human person seeks to realize its true self, there exists a personal morality which is the incarnating of the personal goodness in the world of the subject-person and of humankind. Fuchs' ethics of incarnating the "moral good" introduces the concern of the process in which the human person within one's own historicity endeavors to realize "moral goodness" in order to develop one's own true self. This historical process of realizing the personal good is the fundamental option of the subject-person itself. It is the topic of the next section.

NOTES

1. "Morality, Person and Acts," in *Christian Morality*, p. 106.
2. Ibid., p. 107.
3. Ibid., pp. 108–09.

---

1. Good/bad = Personal subjective moral goodness/badness
   Right/wrong = objectively correct/incorrect action

2. Good = premoral good   bad = premoral evil
   Right = morally good   wrong = personally sinful action
                    Personal moral goodness

3. Morally good actions = objectively correct action
   Morally good person = personal subjective goodness

4. "The 'Sin of the World' and Normative Morality," in *Personal Responsibility*, p. 167.
5. Ibid., p. 154.
6. Ibid., pp. 145–65.
7. See "An Ongoing Discussion in Christian Ethics: 'Intrinsically Evil Acts,'?" in *Christian Ethics*, p. 81. Also "The 'Sin of the World' and Normative Morality," p. 167.
8. "An Ongoing Discussion in Christian Ethics: 'Intrinsically Evil Acts'?" p. 82.
9. Ibid., p. 81.
10. Ibid., p. 82.
11. Ibid., p. 81.
12. "The Sin of the World' and Normative Morality," p. 169. Elsewhere Fuchs expresses this point more clearly by saying that "in the one human action (health care, transplant) the performing of the evil is not an isolated (human) action, but only an element of one action. "The Absoluteness of Behavioral Moral Norms," p. 138.
13. "The 'Sin of the World' and Normative Morality," p. 165.
14. "The Absoluteness of Behavioral Moral Norms," p. 136.
15. Ibid., p. 137.
16. Ibid., p. 138.
17. ". . . I valori esistono, ma nel concreto noon tutti I valori, non in ogni tempo, non in ogni momento della singola vita, sono attuali. Possono perdere o acquistare attualita." "Discussione: Valori, Scrittura, Rivelazione," in *Morale e Coscienza Storica*, p. 70. See also "Storicitá e norma morale," p. 32.
18. "An Ongoing Discussion . . ." p. 82.
19. Ibid., p. 80.
20. Ibid. Examples of moral evils, Fuchs says, "are the readiness to be unjust, unchaste, and unfaithful; also blasphemy, or seducing a person to a sin (that is, to a moral evil)."
21. "Teaching Morality: The Tension between Bishops and Theologians within the Church," in *Christian Ethics*, p. 144.
22. "Affermare la distinzione tra bontá morale della persona e correttezza morale dell'agire . . . non significia che la due realtá distinte siano separate o senza intrinseca relazione l'una con l'altra." "Storicitá e norma morale," p. 22.
23. "Morality: Person and Acts," p. 108.
24. "Infatti, la correttezza dell'agire umano esige di essere accettata ed assunta, nell'agire umano, della moralita personale, cioè dalla bonta morale del soggetto-persona." "Storicita e norma morale," p. 22.
25. "Morality: Person and Acts," p. 108. To acknowledge the difficulty of proving the direct relationship of the rightness of conduct with the personal moral goodness, is not to contradict or to deny the intrinsic relationship of moral goodness with moral rightness.
26. Ibid., p. 117.

Chapter VIII

Fundamental Option

This section is a reflection on the meaning of "fundamental option" with regard to the correlative morality of the right realization of the human person. This reflection on Fuchs' understanding of the "fundamental option" will first being with its historical character with regard to the historical subject-person, then with its practical operation in the present reality of the personal historicity, and finally with its true object for the course of the personal morality. Instead of treating this topic with theological publications, Fuchs suggest that it should be concerned with *Persona humana*, because in this "Declaration," it was the first time for the Council Fathers to comment on the theme of "fundamental option and sin."[1]

The theologians who collaborated in formulating *Persona humana* understood the fundamental option as ". . . the decision which totally commits the person and which is necessary, if mortal sin is to exist; by this option the person, from the depths of the personality, takes up or ratifies a fundamental attitude towards God or people."[2] Namely, fundamental option for these theologians simply means the "direct and formal" acceptance or rejection in the human person of one's love for God and for neighbor. These theologians define the meaning of fundamental option in this way because they defensively stress that "A person . . . sins mortally not only when his action comes from direct contempt for love of God and neighbor, but also when he consciously and freely, for whatever reason, chooses something which is seriously disordered."[3] Fuchs criticizes that this is an erroneous understanding of the fundamental option because it did not grasp the true depth of the human person as such.[4] To understand properly the concept of the fundamental option, the author suggests:

> However, if the human world were viewed as gift and task for humanity and not so much as the human world "under God's commandments" . . . The human

person would then be someone who has conscientiously (certainly, with the aid of Christian grace and "in the light of the Gospel") to discover how the human world of God should be realized so as to better humanity and to correspond to the task bestowed on human persons through creation itself. The self-opening person, that is the loving human person, would seek to carry out what best corresponds to the realization and development of the world. Whenever persons refuse this task in weighty matters, they will be able to discover in the depths of their own self that their behavior stems from a deeply shattered relationship with the Absolute (God, Christ), that is, from a negative fundamental option.[5]

Accordingly, "fundamental option" of Fuchs' ethics is not simply a decision of accepting or rejecting God and people, but rather it is a basic moral task of realizing humanity and the world, which God has bestowed on the subject-person in creation. As having said in previous sections, that the primary imperative of personal conscience is to realize the "personal good" for the right development the human self and the world, and that "incarnating the moral goodness" into the moral rightness as the truly moral actions of the subject-person, there follows that "fundamental option" of Fuchs' ethics belongs primarily to the level of "personal moral goodness." In other words, it is not the categorical choices of concrete actions, but rather the transcendental task of the responsible human person itself. This task can be a positive or negative depending upon whether or not the subject-person seriously acknowledges the "given nature" and one's own "created self," and develops these two realities toward their further right realization.

Thus, "fundamental option" is either positive or negative. There is no third alternation because the human person "always senses the moral obligation of his own historical self-development,"[6] and thereby cannot be arbitrary of one's own being and of the world surrounding. The human person, within its responsible self and basic freedom, either takes up or refuses this basic task for the "well-being" of humanity. Hence, "Morality can approve only those projects and those choices which can be foreseen as successful not only in a particular practical domain, but also in the domain of the *humanum*, which includes all aspects of man's being."[7] If "morality" can approve only the "projects and choices" which entail the success or the well-being of the *humanum*, there follows that true morality is interested only in "positive fundamental option." In one sense, positive "fundamental option" can be understood as the self-disposition of the whole human person, fully being realized in one's innermost core where the subject-person experiences "an Absolute," viz, God. Likewise, negative "fundamental option" can be viewed as the self-withdrawal of the human person as such into one's egoism behind which the subject-person entrenches one's own selfishness.[8] The author affirms that "Naturally, at this point we cannot enter into a more specific discussion of this concept [fundamental option]."⁹ That is to say, there cannot be a deep analysis of the abstract meaning of either positive or negative fundamental option. Granted one puts great effort in analyzing the practical meaning of negative fundamental option, the only conclusion that at which one can arrive is the refusal of the basic moral task or the self-alienation of the selfish egoism. There remains for the present discussion, then, a fitting interest in the practical meaning of positive fundamental option. Another reason why the present discussion should do so is because ". . . the person with his moral goodness can never present himself as he is in his entirety; he manifests himself only in particular acts which, for their part, never touch more than a rather small area of the full horizontal reality of the individual, or of humanity, or of the subhuman world [natural created world]."¹⁰ Namely, fundamental option cannot actualize itself merely in the inner core of the subject-person, but it must be realized in one's acts even though the acts can constitute merely a part of the fullness of human right realization.

If speaking of positive fundamental option as a task of seeking and discovering how the human person and the human world are "to be realized so as to better humanity," there emerges an objection as to when the subject-person should begin one's own responsible fundamental option. This objection is quite legitimate with regard to the historical character of human beings. Fuchs responds that "At the moral level . . . I am not able to act [by] morally referring myself to nature created from the beginning, I just don't know that. I am the man of reality [which] exists today and I ought to find in this reality existing today that thing which for me—image of God, today—is suitable to do."¹¹ In other words, the beginning point of fundamental option is no where other than the presenting existing human person and the present reality which one is facing in experience. The author expresses this point in another way: "Man is always conscious of his identity as a subject, even if he never finds himself as zero point from which to initiate his own history. In every circumstance he perceives himself as coming from the past, from decisions already taken, from a self-realization already begun, from a history of his own which has already shaped him. All of these are not to stop at the present moment, but to decide on how to continue his own history toward his future which has its beginning precisely in the pass, between past and future."¹²

It may seem that the positive "fundamental option" of the subject-person is identical with the historicity of the moral agent itself. This perception, no doubt, is quite correct. The subject-person is an historical and moral being who, within its own capacity of basic freedom and responsible conscience, decides to realize one's own self and to "humanize" the "given world." Inasmuch as such a responsible decision is made, the subject-person begins to incarnate the personal goodness into the right realization of the human world, viz, he or she begins one's own positive fundamental option. In this responsible option, the concept of time should not be reduced to any categorically particular moment or interval of the course of personal history. Rather it must be understood in terms of the past, the future, and the passage of the two. Then in facing present reality, the subject-person must responsibly continue to actualize one's own personal good so much so that the historicity of one's own being can take up its own course. That is to say, the process of incarnating personal good always begins with the challenge of the present reality and continues in its own course until the fullness of the human self and of the humanizing world being reached, viz, until the eschatological realization of the human self.[13] In simple terms, the positive fundamental option of the subject-person is in itself an historical process to the extent that it always begins with the present ensemble of human reality and continues on toward the future of further realization of the human world. Thus, positive fundamental option is nothing other than the humane historicity of the subject-person itself. The historical nature of the positive fundamental option can be more intelligible if one takes into the account that ["In consequence of his historicity as subject, the personal man on the one hand is always himself, on the other hand, in his multiple self-expression in time and space, [the personal man] specifies and changes continuously not only the things of the world object, but truly himself, the subject-person, as well as the richness of being precisely this man who he is."][14]

The historical character of the positive fundamental option in itself is not sufficient to disclose its practical meaning with regard to the humane morality of the subject-person. The inquiry on the operations and the objects of the positive fundamental option will be helpful in this context of the discussion. If the positive fundamental option always has to do with the present ensemble of human reality, and thereby the human person must always bring one's own discernment into the solution corresponding to the challenge of such a present existing reality, there emerges a difficulty of how the subject-person does so without disintegrating the historicity of fundamental option. With regard to this point, the author suggests that " . . . if I must see the reality, then in reality there are diverse possibilities present. This [is] if we consider the man alone as "nature," as "given." But man, with his reason which understands all [of] the complexity of himself, is able to single out which activity corresponds to his whole humanity and which activity does not; it is only the man who is able to do this by means of understanding, evaluating, judging."[15] If the subject-person, within the significant role of one's own reason, must always interpret diverse possibilities of the present reality in order to search out the corresponding solution, the practical function of fundamental option is then meant to be the personal hermeneutical reading of the ensemble of human being. In the simple terms, positive fundamental option is nothing other than the "human personal" intervening the limits and the challenge of the present reality. Yet, if the ensemble of human reality always has to do with premoral values and disvalues due to its embedded "sin-conditioned" character, positive fundamental option must consider the challenge of those values and disvalues as well. Because "Historical man sees himself . . . confronted not only with the reality of the human world, in continuous transformation, but also with norms/codes of multiple behaviors. . ."[16] It is clear that positive fundamental option is the personally responsible intervene of the totality of the challenging present reality which summons the subject-person to project toward the future, viz, toward the fullness of one's own historicity.

Thus, with positive fundamental option the subject-person is able to project one's self toward the future of the true self-development. This is not to say that the fundamental option will enable the subject-person to read hermeneutically all of the possibilities of one's own historicity. As the author admits himself, "We do not know its zero point of departure and neither do we know all the potentialities for our future."[17] Yet, inasmuch as the responsible option begins at the pass of the past and the future, the subject-person must have a serious discernment in order to choose the road of future which one's own discernment individuates. Namely, fundamental option is a morally responsible process in which the subject-person must be able to discern and to project one's own future. Fuchs analyzes the future of human self-development as follows:

> The "future" ["*futuro*"] which man projects and lives is to be distinguished from his definitive "future" ["*avvenire*"]. This latter is not up to the individual to determine; he can and should await it and receive it from that which is already always definitive. Man perceives in fact that his definitive "future" [*definitivo "avvenire"*] is part of the absolute mystery, from which depends, in an analogous way, the very fact of being and of perceiving one's self as man historical and moral. The Christian calls this mystery "God," who in Jesus Christ and in the Spirit calls us to the realization of our history in the direction of [*verso*] a future of ours [*un nostro futuro*] in the time of human history and beyond, in the direction of [*verso*] the promised "future" [*l' "avvenire" promesso*].[18]

Accordingly, the present object of the fundamental option is the "proximate future," in the direction of which the subject-person must always determine oneself from the challenge of the present reality so that one's own historicity can take its course. Yet, such a "proximate future" is not the ultimate future for the moral person. It merely is the humanizing process which will finally aim at the promised future [*l'avvenire promesso*]. This "promised future" for the human person is a part of the absolute mystery which is in the hand of God and beyond the personal capacity of determining. That is why the subject-person should await and receive the "promised future" by means of actualizing the present "proximate future." This is not to say that the promised future is something which can be indifferent to the moral task of the subject-person. It is rather a definitive and ultimate call of the subject-person by God in Jesus and Spirit. The promised future requires the moral person to realize one's temporal history and beyond that which one projects one's self toward the definitive and promised future. Thus, with the positive fundamental option, the subject-person does not merely live the historical moment of one's own historicity, but rather must proceed oneself toward the "definitive absolute" who is God. In the simple terms, the definitive object of the fundamental option is the promised future, which is God's salvation, and which can be successively actualized in the incarnating the "personal good" of the subject-person itself.

In summary, Fuchs' understanding of fundamental option is not an abstract notion which denotes the formal acceptance or rejection of God and people. It is a lifetime task of the historical subject-person, and thereby it is not a simple like categorical act of the human person. As Fuchs explicitly admits it himself, "This call of individual cannot be escaped and can seem a very difficult task." However, the author insists that ". . . both individual and society are constantly prepared for this difficult and inescapable duty."[19] The moral person prepares this task by means of acknowledging the challenge of the present ensemble of human reality, imputing one's own hermeneutical reading of the values and disvalues emerging from the historical moment, and projecting the course of one's historicity toward the promised future, viz, toward the definitive future of God's salvation. The fundamental option is so urgent and mandatory for the subject-person because the self-alienating tendency in the moral person "will continually try to wrest small or great victories,"[20] and because the danger of the personal weakness convincing the acts those which the subject-person "likes or desires are so justifiable and justified."[21]

Since fundamental option is the true and responsible task of the subject-person, it is the only task from which one can live one's own humane morality. Namely, the fundamental option is the truly moral life of the human person who within basic freedom and conscience is responsible for the realization of one's being and the right development of the world surrounding.

NOTES

1. "Our Image of God and Inner Worldly Behavior," p. 30.
2. "Declaration on Certain Questions Concerning Sexual Ethics," (Dec. 29, 1975) (Washington, D.C.: Publications Office USCC, 1976), p. 11.

3. Ibid., p. 12.
4. "Our Image of God and Inner Worldly Behavior," p. 30. In criticizing these theologians' erroneous understanding of the fundamental option, Fuchs, however acknowledges their correct statement of saying that "In reality, it is precisely the fundamental option which in the last resort defines a person's moral disposition." "Declaration on Certain Questions Concerning Sexual Ethics," p. 11.
5. "Our Image of God and Inner Worldly Behavior," p. 32.
6. "... l'uomo-soggetto-persona sempre si percepisce (non dico: si <<riconosce>> in una maniera riflessa o esplicitamente accettata) come un essere morale ... che sempre avverte il compito moral del proprio autosviluppo storico ..." "Storicitá e Norma Morale," p. 19.
7. "Morality as the Shaping of the Future of Man," in *Personal Responsibility*, p. 178.
8. See "Self-realization and Self-alienation," p. 153.
9. "Our Image of God and INnerworldly Behavior," p. 30. The present writer adds the adjectives "abstract" and "practical" to tne term "fundamental option" with the purpose to display Fuchs' thought faithfully on this subject matter. It should be noticed, however, that in this mentioned article Fuchs has not offered any analysis of either abstract or practical meaning of negative fundamental option. The author merely displays the abstractly understanding of many theologians on the positive fundamental option, and he offers his own notion on the practical meaning of positive fundamental option, in which he mentions the practical meaning of negative fundamental option in passing, as the above excerpt indicated. However, this present writer draws Fuchs' though on the negative fundamental option from another article of Fuchs' in order to fulfill the discussion of the concept "fundamental option." The negative fundamental option, either in abstract or practical sense, for Fuchs simply means the self-alienation from God and thereby from one's self, or it signifies the self-withdrawal, self-contradiction, that is the tendency of the selfish self which makes the subject-person become self-alienated. As the author puts it more explicitly, "Sin means self-alienation and hence the arrogant refusal of true self-realization." See "Self-realization and Self-alienation," pp. 151–52.
10. "Morality: Person and Acts," pp. 116–17.
11. "A livello morale ... non posso agire moralmente riferendomi alla natura create delle origini, che neppure conosco. Sono l'uomo della realtá oggi esistente, e debbo trovare in questa realtá oggi esistente che cosa per me—imagine di Dio, oggi— é conveniente fare." "Discussione: Natura, Storia, Moralitá," p. 46.
12. "L'uomo è sempre cosciente della sua identitá come soggetto, anche se non si trova mai in un punto zero, dal quale iniziare la propria storia. In ogni istante egli si percepisce come proveniente da un suo passato, da decisioni giá prese, da una autorealizzazione giá iniziata, dunque da una sua storia che lo ha giá modellato. Tutto questo non per fermarsi nell'istante presente, ma per decidere su come continuare la propria storia verso il suo futuro, il quale ha il suo inizio precisamente nel trapasso tra passato e futuro." "Storicitá e Norma Morale," p. 18.
13. See, e.g., "Self-realization and Self-alienation," p. 150.
14. "In conseguenza della sua storicitá di soggetto l'uomo personale da una parte è sempre se stesso, dall'altra, nel suo esprimersi molteplice nel tempo e nello spazio,

specifica e cambia continuamente non solo qualcosa del mondo oggetto, ma veramente se stesso, soggetto-persona, come pure la ricchezza dell'essere proprio quest'uomo che egli è." "Storicitá e Norma Morale," p. 16.

15. ". . . se devo vedere la realtá, allora nella realtá sono presenti diverse possibilitá. Questo se consideriamo l'uomo solo come << natura >>, << dato >>. Ma l'uomo, con la sua ragione che conosce tutta la complessitá di se stesso, può individuare quale attivitá è ora corrispondente alla sua intera umanitá, e quale attivitá non lo è: e questo solo l'uomo lo può fare, attraverso il capire, valutare, giudicare." "Discussione: Natura, Storia, Moralitá," p. 47.

16. "L'uomo storico si deve. . . confrontato non soltanto con la realtá del mondo umano, in continua trasformazione, ma ánche con norme/codici di comportamento molteplici. . ." "Storicitá e Norma Morale," p. 25.

17. Ibid., p. 20. "Noi non ne conosciamo il punto zero di partenza, e neppure ne conosciamo tutte le potenzialitá per il nostro futuro."

18. Ibid., p. 19. "il << futuro >> che l'uomo progetta e vire va distinto dal suo definitivo << avvenire >>. Quest'ultimo non è il singolo a determinardo: egli può e deve attenderlo e riceverlo da ciò che è giá sempre definitivo. L'uomo percepisce, infatti, che il suo definitivo << avvenire >> fa parte del mistero assoluto, dal quale dipende, in maniera analoga, lo stesso fatto di essere e percepirsi uomo storico e morale. Il cristiano chiama questo mistero << Dio>>, il quale in Cristo Gesù e nello Spirito ci chiama alla realizzazione della nostra storia verso un nostro futuro nel tempo della storia umana e, più oltre, verso l' << avvenire >> promesso." Notice the difference of the noun "*futuro*" and the infinitive "avvenire," both of which in Italian as well as in English mean "future." From the context of the excerpt, one can distinguish the meaning of these two terms in this way: "futuro" means the state of being the future insofar as it is the future, whereas "avvenire" denotes the process of working toward future insofar as it has become future. To put it simply, "*futuro*" means "proximate future," that is in the process of coming to and of participating in the definitive futre [*avvenire*] which is the "promised coming" of God in Jesus Christ.

19. Ibid., p. 17. "Questa chiamata del singolo è ineludibile, e può sembrare un compito difficilissimo. Tuttavia, sia il singolo, sia la societá, si sono costantemente preparati per questo dovere arduo e inderogabile."

20. "Self-realization and Self-alienation," p. 150.

21. "Morality: Person and Acts," p. 114.

Bibliography

Fuchs, Josef. *Natural Law A Theological Investigation.* New York: Sheed and Ward, 1965.
Theology Digest, 14 (Winter 1966), "Sin and Conversion."
Human Values and Christian Morality. Dublin: Gill and Macmillan Ltd., 1970.
Personal Responsibility & Christian Morality. Washington, D.C.: Georgetown University Press, 1983.
Christian Ethics in a Secular Arena. Washington, D.C.: Georgetown University Press, 1984.
Theology Digest, 32 (Fall 1985), "Control over Human Life? Bioethical questions today."
Theology Digest, vol. 33, number 3, Fall 1986. "Marital love: Christian pluralism in the 12th century."
Christian Morality: The Word Becomes Flesh. Washington, D.C.: Georgetown University Press, 1987.
Theology Digest, vol 35, number 3, Fall 1988. "Is there a Catholic Medical Moral?"
"The Absolute in Morality and the Christian Conscience." Unpublished article.
"Conscience and Conscientious Fidelity." Unpublished article.
"Ethical Problems in Christian Prayer of the Psalms." Unpublished article.
"Historicity and Moral Norm." Unpublished article.
"Spiritual Foundations of the Structural Change in Society." Unpublished article.
"Structures of Sin." Unpublished article.

About the Author

Reverend David M. O'Leary, S.T.L., D.Phil., is the University Chaplain at Tufts University. He lectures in the Department of Comparative Religion on the Medford campus and guest lectures on Medical Ethics on the Boston and Grafton campuses.

Reverend O'Leary was born and grew up in Lynn, Massachusetts. He received his B.A. and M.Div. from Saint John's Seminary in Boston. He earned a M.Ed. from Boston College and the S.T.L. degree (Licentiate in Sacred Theology) from Weston Jesuit School of Theology in Cambridge, Massachusetts. He completed his Doctorate in Medical Ethics from the University of Oxford in England. Before coming to Tufts University, Reverend O'Leary was a Professor of Moral Theology, Spirituality and Sexual Ethics at Saint Mary's Seminary & University in Baltimore, Maryland.

Reverend O'Leary reports directly to the President of the University on all religious and spiritual life issues and is the administrator of historic Goddard Chapel. He does work in spiritual direction, retreats, pastoral counseling, engaged and marriage counseling and the full range of campus ministry at Tufts University. He is also the Chair of the Institution Review Board for human subjects research and a member of the IRB for the Tufts New England Medical Center in Boston. He is also a member of the Harvard Board of Ministry, Memorial Church, Harvard University.

He has been featured in the Boston Sunday Globe and written up for his pioneering Comparative Religion course "Catholicism in Crisis." He has been interviewed on radio and television on a variety of religious and spiritual issues. He is a member of the American Academy of Religion, the Catholic Theological Society of America and the North American Inter Faith Network. He has published articles on spirituality and an op-ed piece in the Boston

Globe, "When Adults Become Abusers of Young People." (Boston Globe, July 11, 2000) as well as the following books:

Roman Catholic Beliefs and Prayers, A Handbook for those on a Spiritual Journey

Seeking the Path of God's Justice, An Analysis of the U.S. Bishops' Pastoral Letter on Economic Justice

The Roman Catholic Perspective on the Morality of Withdrawing or Withholding Food and Fluid Administered Artificially to an Individual in the Persistent Vegetative State

www.ingramcontent.com/pod-product-compliance
Lightning Source LLC
Chambersburg PA
CBHW021134300426
44113CB00006B/431